Human A Different Way:

Resurrect Christ Within

Boston Carter, Ph.D.

Elemental Publishing
Monroe, Washington. USA

Publisher:
Elemental Publishing
Monroe, WA 98272

Copyright © 2025 Boston Carter

All rights reserved. No part of this publication may be reproduced or transmitted in any form or by any means, electronic or mechanical, including photo-copying, recording, or by any information storage and retrieval system, without permission in writing from Elemental Publishing.

Archedomi® is a registered trademark of Elemental Research and Consulting Group, LLC. The term may not be used outside of reference to the model and the work of Boston Carter.

Visit: HumanADifferentWay.com
ISBN: 978-1-7320763-3-4

Elemental Publishing is owned by
Elemental Research and Consulting Group, LLC
Cover design by Boston Carter
Cover photo from Pixabay. Artist unnamed. The white Easter Lilly represents the resurrection.

For everyone who wants to be in this world, but not of it.

Human A Different Way:

Resurrect Christ Within

Boston Carter, Ph.D.

Introduction	**11**
About Boston Carter	**15**
What to Expect	**19**
Part One: Philosophical Foundations	**21**
Duality	21
Opposites	21
Fractals	24
Archetypes	25
Consciousness	27
Instinct	27
Instinct and Intuition	29
Victim	30
Saboteur	32
Part Two: The Archedomi® Model	**33**
Water	37
Exercise 1:	37
Exercise 2:	39
Exercise 3:	39
Exercise 4:	41
Exercise 5:	41
Exercise 6:	42
Exercise 7:	42
Exercise 8:	43
Exercise 9:	44
Exercise 10:	45
Exercise 11:	46
Fire	47
Exercise 12:	50
Exercise 13:	51
Exercise 14:	52
Exercise 15:	52
Exercise 16:	53
Exercise 17:	53
Exercise 18:	54

Earth	55
Exercise 19:	55
Exercise 20:	56
Exercise 21:	56
Exercise 22:	58
Exercise 23:	58
Exercise 24:	59
Exercise 25:	60
Exercise 26:	61
Air	62
Exercise 27:	63
Exercise 28:	65
Exercise 29:	65
Exercise 30:	66
Exercise 31:	66
Exercise 32:	67
Part Three: Wholeness	**69**
Functions	70
Part 4: Intuition	**77**
Projection vs. Intuition	77
Communications: Preparation	79
Presence and Gratitude:	79
Meditations	80
Communications: To and From Higher Self	81
Ask the right questions.	81
Trusting the Answers	82
Imaginal Tools	84
Sudden Thoughts, Feelings, or Visions	85
Archetypes and Symbols/Images	86
Synchronicity	88
Dreams	89
Numbers	90
Illness/physical or emotional changes	91
Knowledge: Filters of information flow	93
Energy Work	94

Feeling energy with your hands	95
Feeling energy with your emotions	96
Feeling energy with your body	96
Seeing energy with your eyes	97
Seeing energy like a memory	98
Seeing energy with imagination	98
Sending energy	99
Sending energy with permission	99
Sending energy with feelings and images	100
Receiving energy	101
Agreement, Shields, and Grounding	101
Instructing your body	103
Part 5: Summary of Mastery	**105**
Some symptoms of mastery:	105
Activity Suggestions	106
Appendix A: Thinking Words	**109**
Appendix B: Feeling Words	**111**
Appendix C: The Enneagrid (not Enneagram)	**113**
Glossary	**119**
Bibliography	**123**

Introduction

In his original Aramaic language, Yeshua (Jesus) referred to two parts of self, Naphsha and Ruha. Naphsha refers to the lower self, or what I call instinct, and Ruha the higher self. The two connect through the heart center. A Semitic saying during Yeshua's time is "With only one eye we get a limited, two-dimensional view. With two eyes, we have a three-dimensional view. When we reconcile them, it's as though we have access to all dimensions".[1] This saying reflects the reconciliation of Naphsha and Ruha conveyed to us by Yeshua, which is the crux of his teachings. What was he talking about and how do we do it?

When a human being is born, the first breath is drawn. That first breath begins your journey. Your higher self (son of God) becomes shrouded from awareness as your soul entangles with the planet's dualistic energy system.[2] You become dominated by the instinct mind (son of man/Naphsha/lower self) that perceives through the binary energy dynamic of Gaia, our mother Earth.

How do you reconcile instinct and higher self to become whole while still in the body? On the instinct side, there are specific things to do. Doing them raises your self-value, which is the first step to forming a reconciliation. The instinct perceptions have

> "Therefore if any man be in Christ [*higher self*], he is a new creature: old things are passed away; behold, all things are become new" (King James Bible. 2 Corinthians, 5:17). *This verse may suggest that reconciliation of the two sides can occur while incarnate. One becomes new, or is reborn when higher self is accessed.*

---

[1] Douglas-Klotz, 2022. 20.
[2] Muranyi, 2013. 188.

patterns to them that cause all the pain and suffering that exists in the world. Built into those patterns are specific gateways that lead to reconciliation and return to wholeness.

Here are four instinct themes that people are born to. Understanding how these work to keep your higher self out of awareness opens the door to wholeness. This may be new for you. Allow yourself to be a little confused for a bit. It will come together. Allow yourself to cry when you see yourself in the patterns. Allow yourself to feel anxious with questions. They will be answered. Allow yourself to think "this isn't true of me". You may see it differently later.

Do one or more of the following four descriptors sound like you, especially in your youth?

1. Water types may have a recurring experience of rejection with a constant longing for one other person to love you no matter what. Recurring rejection is accompanied by painful feelings of unworthiness and not being seen. If this is you, know that you are not fated to be alone. This is fixable.
2. Air types may have a recurring experience of fearing anger and conflict. Others' anger may feel like you are about to be abandoned. You may worry about everything, including being alone. Conflict seems to find you constantly. You may feel anxiety, often seeing the worst-case scenario, guilt, shame, and overwhelming responsibility. If this is you, know that there is a way to end all of it.
3. Earth types may have a recurring experience of wanting to be at home. Going out into the world means that you likely go to the same grocery store, gas station, restaurant, and order the same food that you always do. You also might have trouble with papers on many

horizontal surfaces in your home; not knowing what to do with them. You may generally not like people very much, and you long to understand God and the universe. You may suffer from loneliness and not knowing enough. If this is you, it can change if you want it to. You may not want it to.
4. Fire types may have a recurring experience of feeling betrayed. You might prefer to be the center of attention and have others adapt to your needs. You might not understand why people won't commit to you, or why it's so hard for them to give you what you want. You may struggle with a constant need for more stuff, more attention, and a lack of trusting anyone or God. This can change.

These four templates represent patterns of instinct, often referred to as ego. They create a specific perspective that can feel like fate has set you up for a difficult situation. Your theme was given to you as a tool for survival and evolution. In the following pages, you'll learn about your template(s), how they keep you focused on the instinct perspective, which causes pain and suffering, and how to begin reconciliation. You have the power and authority to do this once you understand how it works.

Before I tell you about the template-themed patterns of instinct, I'd like to tell you about me so you have an idea of who is speaking to you, and how I came to this information.

About Boston Carter

Around 1997, in my early thirties, I started noticing something strange about myself. Here is what happened: I had recently come across an ad in a spiritual newspaper that was looking for people to join a discussion group about two specific metaphysical books. I had read both books with great enthusiasm and was eager to chat about them. Two women had put up the ad, making us a group of three since I was the only one who had responded to it.

One of the women was psychic. She'd often share her gifts, and we started chatting about energy and consciousness. At one meeting, she mentioned a stomach pain. Without thinking, I sensed the energy in her stomach and told her I could see it and what it was about. She looked at herself and then at me, saying, "I see. What are you going to do about it?" I was surprised by her suggestion that I could do anything about it, but I thought, okay, I'll see what it needs. I 'talked' to the pain, asked what it needed, and gave it love energy. The pain vanished.

This was my awakening to being a Medical Intuitive. If I hadn't been in such a supportive environment that already believed in energy as real, I may never have known about this natural gift. I started doing free readings for friends who were up for it, so I could practice. I learned how to tell their true energy apart from my own, how to ask the right questions of the energy, and to trust the answers that came back, even if I had to say, 'I'm not sure'. My favorite experience is when I get information that I never would have thought of myself. Then I know for sure my ego isn't making it up. I've also learned that there's a feeling associated with truth. Truth feels like a beautiful sunset. It brings a sense of peace and completion, like there's nowhere else to go. It's like the energy is saying, 'I've reached the end of my inquiry and no information is missing.'

Over time, I became really good at what I did. I started offering readings to people and helping naturopathic doctors figure out tricky cases. To be honest, I did this full-time because the housing market crashed when I made my living as a carpenter. I didn't have any other skills. I wanted to help people understand their health problems. I could talk to those problems and figure out why they were there in the first place. About 80% of the time, those problems had repeating thoughts and feelings that were causing the illness. There's no judgment here. Everyone manages their energy to affect their health, but most haven't been taught how to do it well. If you're sick, it's not your fault. Learn what you can and do what you can. No blame. After a few years of doing this full-time, I wanted to find a better way to help. Telling people what their problems were wasn't enough because what I saw inside them was so much more powerful.

My intuitive work taught me that people are manifestation engines. Thoughts and feelings of the mental and emotional planes affect the physical plane. This understanding led me to discover patterns to people's thoughts, feelings, and behaviors. I "downloaded" through intuition, the instinct patterns of perception and structured them into a model that I now call Archedomi® (from two Greek words: Arche, meaning original or ancient, and domi, meaning structure). I realized that I did not have the language to express what I understood. I needed greater knowledge to give voice to what I saw.

My Ph.D. in depth psychology gave me some solid tools to explain what I see in people. However, the Archedomi model is not a formal academic study, which is perfectly fine with me. My audience isn't academia; it's you. You can decide if this resonates with you. I have no stake in your belief in me or your acceptance of Archedomi. My goal is to share the results of my work so this significant information is available to help you.

I'm an intuitive practitioner who can tap into the collective unconscious to gather insights. I'm not perfect, but I've been observing people through this model for 25 years, and it seems consistently accurate. I've made adjustments over time to make it clearer or more understandable, and there are other ways to structure this information that would still be valid. My perspective is just one of many potentials.

> "Mystics are people who have a particularly vivid experience of the processes of the collective unconscious. Mystical experience is experience of archetypes."
> Jung, C. G. (1935). [CW], Vol. 18. para. 218.

The journey of self-discovery and personal growth is intimate and should be approached only when you're ready. There is no rush and no judgment. I've been on this path myself, and I know it can be tough. My intuition and knowledge came later in life, and it didn't stop me from making mistakes. I was a total mess as a kid, young adult, and even older adult. It took me a long time to figure out basic things, and I'm still learning. But maybe that's what drives me to share this knowledge. Understanding the psychology of your soul can make everything so much easier.

What to Expect

From the depths of being, consciousness gives life force, health, and lived experiences. To explain this, I'll use terms like archetypes, shadow, and complex from Dr. Carl Jung. I'll explain them as I first use them. I'll also include terms from other sources, like the Hindu concept of Chakras, which are energy centers in the body. These centers control different types of energy that then nourish our cells. Each gland is like a transfer station for the energy center it's connected to. For example, I remember a woman with a metabolic condition because of her thyroid, which is connected to the throat chakra. When I 'talked' to the blocked energy in her thyroid, I asked it to give me a statement. The statement was, "I never get to do what I want." That's the thought/feeling energy that's stuck in her thyroid. The throat chakra is responsible for the energy category of will or volition. This woman had a lifelong feeling of not being able to exercise her own will or volition, which created a blockage of energy flow in her thyroid.

I'll share some insights into how humans function, our inner workings, the patterns of thoughts, feelings, and addictive behaviors that can lead to illness and relational suffering. These patterns keep us from reaching our true potential, our sacred and divine home, a place of love and multidimensional power that brings inner peace and balance.

My goal is to guide you back home without sacrificing your physical form. Home is a state of complete consciousness, meaning a deep connection to everything and everyone. It's a place of peace and trust in life and yourself. It is a state of heaven. To be in this world, but not of it, is to hold heaven on earth. I'll describe the attributes of this mastery later on.

I'm a bit of a structuralist. I like to organize information in a logical and systematic way. I created the Archedomi® model to explain how people interact with each other, what causes problems in those interactions, and what solutions can be found. I'll also explain why it works that way. That's all coming up in the Archedomi section, Part 2.

You will find in gray boxes some notes that refer to the reading. Along the way, I make some comparisons between what Yeshua (Jesus) said we should do and what the Archedomi model shows are gateways out of instinct mind. Within those boxes, I may expand on some ideas. My ideas are in italics.

Part One: Philosophical Foundations

Duality

When you're born, something incredible happens. You draw your first breath. This single act completes the four elements of body (earth), spirit (fire), emotions (water), and intellect (air). Welcome back. You are a soul incarnate belonging to an energy system that is entangled with the earth's energy system. The result is a veiled awareness – a separation from your whole self that follows patterns or themes that work within the natural confines of duality that is the earth's energy system.

Opposites

When your awareness entangles with the earth's energy, you get a pattern of instinct perception (small self, or son of man) that shrouds your awareness into a two-dimensional system of opposites because the earth's energy system is binary.[3]

> The book of Genesis 2:9 tells of the "tree of life also in the midst of the garden, and the tree of knowledge of good and evil" (King James Bible). *In my view, the tree of life is higher self, while the tree of knowledge of good and evil, depicting duality, represents instinct. In this way, Genesis may be a symbolic parable of human consciousness.*

The instinct mind resides in duality, perpetuating the opposites and their conflictual function. It's this instinct part of the psyche that causes pain and suffering because it sees life as separate from everything else. When in whole consciousness, everything is balanced among all energy dynamics. People are connected to the planet's dualistic energy system, and as we grow, so does the planet. It's like the 100th monkey theory. The more people become consciously whole, the more others will follow suit, and it all

---
[3] Dr. Carl Jung founded his work on the concept of opposites. Lao Tzu also wrote of this phenomenon in terms of Yin and Yang.

happens through the planet's energy system. As you work on this, you're helping the world heal and evolve.

Imagine two ideas that are constantly at odds, like a rubber band stretched taut. You pull and pull, and eventually, it snaps. That breaking point is called a transcendent function. When two opposing ideas can't find a way to agree, they build tension like that rubber band and break through to a new idea, a new level of conscious functioning. When you see a conflict arise this way, and the two sides can't find a solution, tension builds. This is true for both groups and individuals.

On the individual level, conflict arises when our ideal self clashes with our real self. We strive to live up to our ideal selves, but when we can't or don't, we confront our real selves and feel the tension between them. This tension can manifest as anger, depression, anxiety, or other negative emotions. We can either ignore the milder tensions or work towards a breakthrough. Sometimes, when the need for change remains hidden or denied, external events occur as symbolic representations of the inner conflict. Examples include major illnesses, car accidents, relationship endings, or other significant life changes. If we ignore our inner conflicts, breakthroughs happen, as if fate is against us. This process isn't about fault or blame; it's simply how things work. It's impossible to avoid all negative events, as they serve a purpose for our souls. The mundane aspects of life are tools in our soul's journey.

Athletes are a great example of this. Their sport is all about the mental game - what they think and feel. If they stay focused and not too worried about what others think, they do great. But if they're too attached to winning or making their success about themselves, they often mess up. The task is to stay in the present moment. That's true for everyone.

Let me give you a more specific example. A client was camping in her van at a rest stop, and during the night, someone hit the rear left corner of her van, leaving a big dent. They quickly drove away. Vehicles represent how we journey through life. They carry us and bring us back home. The fact that the rear left side was hit (the yin/yin or unconscious blind spot, symbolically speaking) suggests that there's something the person is unaware of. So, we take a closer look. It was dark, and the driver of the other vehicle probably couldn't see the van clearly. My client has an internal struggle between her ideal (whole) self, which is comfortable and ready to be seen, and her real (instinct) self, which wants to stay hidden. These two sides in conflict create tension. If one remains unaware of a mounting tension, it can manifest in the outer world. In this case, her van was hit. This incident became an awareness of the conflict, if one chooses to see it. When I mentioned that she doesn't like to be seen, she realized that she even created an energy barrier around her van to make herself invisible to others, as a way of protecting herself. It worked! Of course, some things are mere coincidence, or not knowable, but always worth looking at.

Imagine two opposing ideas. They can't coexist, so they must change or evolve into something new. When our psyche uses opposites (instinct mind), the new idea is usually the opposite of another concept, leading to persistant conflicts, even though the new idea feels good for a while. When problems are solve using opposites, we often end up creating more problems. This is especially true when people think solutions are either "my way" or "your way."

Fractals

What do fractals have to do with psyche and patterns of instinct? Science has discovered that most natural shapes are actually created through fractals. Fractals are simple equations that reiterate to create rough and irregular shapes, like rocks, trees, coastlines, mountains, even the human nervous system and circulatory system. Reiteration is when the solution to an equation is put back into the same equation to get a new solution. Doing this thousands or millions of times creates the shapes of nature.

When you work out a fractal shape to its root equation, such as $ax^2 + bx + c = 0$, you can see the simplicity of it. One equation creates whole mountain ranges. The reiteration process is a linear pattern that gives it complexity, shape, and imagery. Given that the human instinct is entangled with the earth (nature), might it be that veiled consciousness of instinct is also created by fractals? If so, wouldn't they also have a simple root like the quadratic equation? Perhaps one based in 2^x like when a human egg is fertilized and cellular division creates a whole new person? One cell becomes two, then four, then eight, and so on.

> "And a river went out of Eden to water the garden; and from thence it was parted, and became into **four** heads" (King James Bible. Genesis: 2:10). *This verse immediately follows the verse on the tree of life and the tree of knowledge of good and evil. Out of the one garden comes two trees, and then four rivers, like fractals of 2^x. Viewed symbolically, earth may be the garden, the two trees are the incarnated function of psyche, and the four rivers flowing from the earth may be the instinct patterns that derive from the tree of knowledge of good and evil (duality). The tree of life remains whole.*

What if the instinct patterns of perception within psyche could be worked out to their root equations?

The "equation" you're born with is your instinct. I see it as a template, like an equation, that shapes your thoughts, feelings, and behaviors. There are four basic templates of instinct, and I use the symbols of fire, earth, air, and water to represent them. The ancient Greek philosopher Empedocles first used these element symbols to describe the four core attributes of everything.[4] I use them because they work well in a symbolic way, which I'll explain later.

Why am I bringing fractals into this discussion? I could leave them out, but there's one important thing about them and the human psyche. Fractals are self-similar images - no matter how big you make them, the shapes stay the same. From the tiniest microbe to the biggest galaxy, they're the same. In the human mind, instincts aren't just personal, they're also shared by all of us. They are cultural, as well as individual, in all their varying degrees of influence, like a fractal. And we're all products of nature, subject to its laws of formation. Gaia is the mother of your veiled awareness (instinct). Individuals deal with opposites and so do groups. This is visible in political, social, and economic systems. There may be more than two political parties, but each party will reflect instinct pattern(s) in its ideology. You may see this as you wend your way through the discussion of the pattern types.

Archetypes

Fractals create shapes and images that become

> "I call these structures archetypes because they function in a way similar to instinctual patterns of behaviour."
> (Jung, C. G. 1957. [CW vol. 3], para. 549.)

---
[4] Campbell, G. (n.d.).

universal symbols. Archetypes are structuring patterns that belong to the collective unconscious and emerge into awareness as an image of some kind.[5] Because they are collective, they belong to all people regardless of race, region, or religion. The fact that they do belong to all people means that archetypal images are from the soul level. That is why we study them and use them to "see" into the unaware part of the psyche. Some archetype examples: no matter who you are, or where you're from, you will understand about time, mother, father, child, rocks, water, air, fire, earth, and so much more. Magician, joker, wise old man, are to name a few more. These archetypes show up in personalities, in nature, and everywhere.

Archetypes and fractals are related in the sense that both emerge into being as shapes and images. They may be closely related, but I have no evidence of that. For example, I refer to the previous story of the client whose van was damaged during the night by another vehicle. The client's inner conflict between ideal self that wants to be seen and real self that wants to be invisible emerged onto the physical plane as an archetypal event of an "accident" that struck the symbolically unaware portion of her van. When the event is viewed through the archetypal, or symbolic, lens, a deeper understanding can be obtained.

Here's another way to look at archetypes: People unconsciously show their archetypal traits in the world around them. One way this happens is through art. I know a woman who had a lot of art in her house. Her favorite painting was of a young girl with a sad face and tears streaming down her cheeks. She also had several figurines of children with tears on their faces. This woman had a lot of

---

[5] Jung, C. G. (1990).

emotions, but her parents weren't very emotional. So, she felt sad, alone, and out of place. She put those feelings into her art. You could see the signs of a neglected child archetype all over her house.

I've seen similar projections in people who might have a favorite movie. Take this young woman, for example. She was adopted and didn't really bond with her new parents. This attachment disorder caused her a lot of pain. But guess what? Her favorite movie was Bambi. The story of a young fawn who loses its mother resonated with her on a deep level. The abandoned child archetype plays out in this story and in her story.

Archetypes are super helpful in understanding how they influence our thoughts, feelings, and behaviors without us even realizing it. They're also common in dreams, but I won't go into that in detail here. If you're interested, it's definitely worth checking out!

Consciousness

Usually, we think of consciousness as what we know or feel. But I see it differently. I believe consciousness is the underlying energy that connects everything in the universe. It's infinite and fills the entire field of existence. In my opinion, consciousness is what makes you a soul, while your awareness can be hidden or obscured. Awareness is where your attention is focused. It's important to note that there's still a lot of debate among experts in different fields about consciousness being the all, or everything.

Instinct

I believe that human awareness is shrouded, or veiled, by incarnation, and that people are in the process of evolving out of that shroud, returning to wholeness. I believe this because I can "see" somewhat metaphysically. I could cite people with doctorate degrees who claim as I do, and still others would claim against it. I don't see the value of that so I'll simply say that this is my belief based on my experiences. Your beliefs and experiences may be different. Take the parts of my beliefs that you like, and leave the parts that don't work for you.

The instinct mind functions in fractal lenses— a system of thinking and perceiving that typically limits our solution options to two: fight or flight, us and them, win or lose. Given that a straight line connects two ends, this two-dimensional system may also contribute to the human sense of linearity and structure.

In survival situations, quick thinking is crucial. You don't have time to weigh options. You just react. In this way, two-dimensional thinking is beneficial to survival. But if you stay in this mindset even when you need to think critically, you actually make things worse. Thinking in terms of 'us' and 'them,' 'win' or 'lose,' can leave someone without what they need, and that's a problem. Competition for resources means many go without.

Instinct is a survival mechanism that helps us perceive the world, but it can be a bit scary and lead to fear-based decisions. When faced with two choices, one or the other can trigger fear in someone because they might feel like things are going wrong if they don't get their way. They might feel powerless to achieve what they want. This perspective can make compromise seem threatening.

Instinct craves power. It's a natural mechanism because having power means controlling resources. Wholeness doesn't care about power because it already has it and knows it. Feeling disconnected from wholeness, instinct believes it's powerless, which is why it seeks power. When someone feels powerless in a situation, like "I never get to do what I want," they're in victim mode. If they can't do what they want, they think it's because someone else has the power to stop them. Often, people give away their power, letting someone else control what they do and when. Giving away personal power and authority is okay sometimes, but it's important to be aware and intentional about it. I am not saying that not getting what you want makes you a victim. I am saying that how you see it makes you a victim. See it as betrayal, rejection, or abandonment, then you're a victim. See it as spirit redirecting you, then you trust in higher self to know more than you about what's going on.

> *Consider this: What if sin doesn't mean immorality? What if sin means fear? To be born of sin may mean to be born afraid because the separation of consciousness into a dominating instinct is meant to keep you afraid for physical survival. Instinct is duality and fear-based. We do bad things because of fear. To "sin no more" may be to surrender fears and open the heart center as a move toward wholeness, or higher self.*
>
> Yeshua:
> "Let not your heart be troubled, neither let it be afraid". (King James Bible. John 14:27).
>
> Buddha:
> "May I abide transcending fear and dread" (Nanamoli, B. & Bodhi, B., 2005, p. 113).

Instinct and Intuition

While I'm on the topic of instinct, I want to make a quick distinction between it and intuition. This term is often interchanged in equal measure with intuition. In my view, these are two distinctly different things. Instinct is the pattern of perception that promotes physical survival and operates through the two-dimensional lens of Earth's dualistic energy system. Intuition is communication with higher self that accesses whole consciousness and multi-dimensional reality of the metaphysical realm. For example, if you are walking down the street and feel a sudden urge to cross it, unknowingly to avoid a stranger lurking nearby, that is intuition telling you to change locations for safety. Instinct tells you to be scared about it when you realize what just happened.

Instinct has four templates of perception that will be described in the next section on the Archedomi® model. Any of those four patterns combine with some common archetypal motifs to create fear-based thinking. The most common archetypal motifs are victim and saboteur.[6]

> "I am a victim of birth, ageing, and death, of sorrow, lamentation, pain, grief, and despair; I am a victim of suffering, a prey to suffering. Surely an ending of this whole mass of suffering can be known." (Buddha, Nanamoli, B. & Bodhi, B., 2005, p. 284).

Victim

Most people believe that childhood shapes our lives. For instance, someone might tell their therapist about their mother leaving them when they were three and how that makes them fear abandonment. Or, they might say that their father always

---
[6] Myss, C. (2013)

yelled and that's why they hate conflict. I can't deny that your upbringing and environment can affect your feelings. They do, but there's another factor that I think causes more of the typical angst than we realize. It's your instinct pattern of perception. Have you ever wondered why one child in a family struggles with fear of abandonment, while another is set off by a know-it-all? Weren't they raised by the same people? If those who raised you were the only ones responsible for your wounded perspective, wouldn't all children in the household have the same wound?

The victim archetype is often seen alongside the hero and villain. They're like the instinct's classic trio, driven by survival. It's common to tell a story in therapy where you might be the hero, and the person you're struggling with (often your parents) could be the villain. This perception is part of instinct's way of protecting itself. It's the 'us vs. them' duality at play. Instinct wants to stay the hero so it doesn't have to change anything. If you figure out that instinct is making you a victim unnecessarily, it could lose its power and even die. Instinct wants to survive, so it gives you a perception of the archetypal trio that helps it stay alive. But instinct is like a parasite that sucks the life out of you if you don't remove it.

A victim mindset is often rooted in instinct's fear-based perceptions and feelings of powerlessness. If you feel powerless to _____, then you might see yourself as a victim of someone else's control over you. When you tell your story, you might shift between portraying yourself as a hero and as a victim.

The victim archetype makes one think that their parents, or someone else, created their primary issues. It wants to blame someone else. The truth is that this person who feels abandoned was always going to have issues with abandonment because they're an air type. I'll get into that more later on, but know that the victim archetype is prominent in the instinct mind.

Saboteur

The next most prominent archetype that operates through instinct is the saboteur. It uses the two-dimensional conflicts of opposites within you to prevent success. Addictive behavioral, feeling, and thinking patterns rooted in your instinct are at the core of your self-sabotage. You might not even realize you're self-sabotaging. It's just how people are. Instinct is the norm. Seeing it clearly can be tough. Take an air type person, for example. They may feel like a victim of their perceived wound - fear of abandonment. But here's the thing: they might be the one causing their own abandonment. Because air types fear separation, they avoid conflict. They often don't tell the whole truth (addictive behavior) because they fear people getting upset with them. But then others find out the truth and get angry. The air type person sees this as proof that they were right to keep a secret. They might feel victimized by the other person's anger. But they're not really a victim. They're self-sabotaging. I'll dive deeper into this in part 2.

Sometimes, we unintentionally create problems for ourselves. Instead of beating yourself up, try to figure out what you did to contribute to the issue and what you can do differently next time. Everyone has their own struggles and habits, and it's okay to not be perfect. Instinct likes for you to take things personally.

Part Two: The Archedomi® Model

"Any energy that would repeat itself over and over again . . . is dark energy[7]. . . in the discovery of light, darkness cannot exist.[8]"

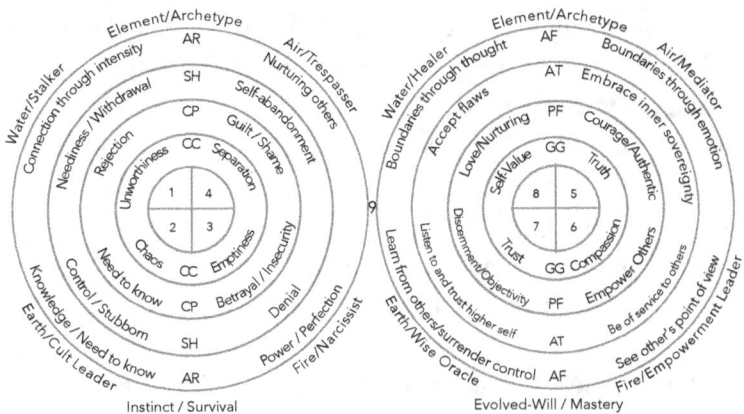

CC: Core Complex
CP: Core Perception
SH: Shadow
AR: Addictive Response

AF: Awareness Focus
AT: Action Task
PF: Positive Force
GG: Gift of Grace

The Archedomi model explains how our instincts create repeating patterns of perception that keep us stuck in fear-based thinking (darkness[9]). But when we fully integrate the two sides of instinct and higher self, we experience multi-dimensional consciousness.

---

[7] April 17, 2024: Wednesdays with Kryon. Is There a Real Battle of Dark and Light: Loc. 4:50. Available at https://www.menus.kryon.com/freeaudio

[8] April 23, 2024: Monument Valley Tour. Message 2. Loc. 14:50 Available at https://www.menus.kryon.com/freeaudio

[9] I want to clarify here that I use the term dark because it is the most commonly understood metaphor for the conflict of the duality in which this part of psyche exists. I do not, under any circumstances, condone the relationship of dark energy to dark skinned people. There is none. All people possess dark and light potentials that have nothing to do with skin color. This is a message for our current times and will be completely unnecessary in the future energy dynamics of humanity. That is why it is a footnote. We could replace dark with magnetic and light with electric. This language is a reflection of our dualistic nature and will change in the future.

The left wheel represents the instinct layers of thoughts, feelings, and behaviors, both aware and unaware, that each pattern incorporates. It could be called the Tree of the knowledge of good and evil. The right wheel shows you what to choose instead, so you can focus on mastering it or connecting with your higher self (Ruha), which could also be called the Tree of Life. As you read through the patterns, you might see yourself reflected in them. If you're not sure, I suggest working all the exercises for all the patterns. Some of you have all four equally, while others have them to some degree. As you work through your primary pattern, the others will become more apparent. So, working all four patterns can only help you, but maybe one at a time.

As I mentioned before, our world is like a big dance of opposites. Think of it as a yin-yang, with masculine and feminine, hot and cold, up and down. This dance of opposites is what gives us our instincts, our inner compass.

Suffering occurs due to separation of awareness. You have the power to shift that, specific to your template(s). I add some channeled information here and there from Kryon because that information feels true to me and makes sense with what I've observed. My goal is to give you as much explanation of how consciousness works as possible. Because this is a new concept, some of it may not be completely accurate, but it's the best information available right now. I give it room to grow into something else later on, whether through me or others.

I'll start with the left instinct wheel, going through each layer separately. The left wheel shows the problems, while the right wheel shows the solutions. The goal is to help you understand what drives your template and how to steer yourself away from its chaotic path to misery towards wholeness, from separation to connected mastery.

Before I dive into the instinct templates and worldview lenses, I wanted to share something important. The Core Perception of your template, which is rejection, chaos, separation, or emptiness, is totally changeable. You're not stuck with these themes. Let's get started on making your life better, right now! **Don't take these descriptions as a judgment of yourself or others. Everyone has these.** Your pattern isn't about your worth or value. It's about your task as an incarnate human being to evolve out of it, choosing wholeness.

> *What action can bridge the higher and lower selves as Yeshua did? Where the energies of our two selves meet is in the heart center. To find it, place your index finger where your two collar bones meet at the base of your throat. Then four finger widths down, and two inches (5cm) inside your chest, place your awareness. Your heart-centered awareness in the now moment is your portal to higher self.*

Please spread the word about this work to your friends and family, but be careful not to share your personal insights or assumptions about their patterns. Let them discover their own journey. The goal of this work is to apply it to ourselves (with mastery), not to analyze or fix others unless you're invited to do so and have training to use this information that way.

Offered exercises show you how the instinct templates work. You might have one pattern that's always in your mind, but everyone has all four to some degree. Maybe one dominates more than the others. Some people experience all four equally, most have one or two that they are aware of. You might want to read through all four patterns before doing the exercises, or maybe you don't want to do them at all? You decide what's best for you. If you decide to do the exercises, they'll help you understand others' point of view and your own. Understanding others' point of view is not about analyzing them. It is about being aware of how you react to them. I suggest using a journal to work these exercises because there might be a deeper connection if you write by hand, but if typing is more your thing, that's totally fine too. You know what works best for you.

Yeshua spoke with the idea that those with "ears to hear" would understand the higher meaning of his words. This same was true of alchemy, the ancient science of materialism. Dr. Carl Jung studied alchemy closely because it had been cast aside as ridiculous, which meant that it was left undisturbed and un-reinterpreted over a long period of time. It held within its structures and formulas a projection of the unconscious of its practitioners. For those spiritual adepts with a deeper understanding (ears to hear), the formulas were instructions for spiritual processes, while those with a literal interpretation perceived them as chemical equations. Consider the activity of turning lead into gold. This may be symbolic of turning instinct into higher self. Alchemy states that unity separates into the four elements of fire, earth, air, and water, and it is the adept's task to reunite the elements (Jung, 1967). *This idea is similar to the symbolism found in the book of Genesis: Eden (unity/heaven) houses the two trees and the four rivers.*

Water

Let's take a moment to think about water as a substance. As a single molecule, water cannot be wet. It must bond with other molecules to become what it is meant to be. It has no shape of its own. It spills out into nothingness, where it can dry up into non-existence if not contained properly. Water fills in the lowest spaces first and therefore occupies depths. Water, as a metaphor for perception, creates a Core Complex (CC) of unworthiness because, having no shape, it lacks a distinct identity. Complex, a term coined by Jung, represents an unaware feeling that when activated, appears as a neurosis and makes one act in an irrational way, as if another personality takes over in some way. By gaining deep awareness of this complex, its negative impact can be mitigated. For water type people, the CC of unworthiness drives all of the layers of thoughts, feelings, and behaviors that are shown above on the model's left wheel. For most people, the CC is a feeling that is simply always there. Because it feels so normal, it often resides within an unaware attitude. It remains unnamed, usually until adulthood, unless someone in your life can tell you about it. You may identify so closely with this feeling of low value that questioning its truth may not occur to you.

Becoming the master healer that you are meant to be – a healer with boundaries, self-care, and self-value – requires moving your awareness out of the instinct theme. On the other side of instinct awaits a deeply rich self-love.

Exercise 1:
Take some time to write down what you think about your worth as a person, friend, partner, and member of society. Think about what you want to believe about yourself in each

of these roles. (Appendix A lists some helpful thinking words.) What makes you valuable? By thinking about your roles, you can start sorting your beliefs about yourself. This helps you understand the difference between your real self and your ideal self, and where you might have conflicts. Sorting makes it easier to deal with feelings of unworthiness.

Some of your thoughts and feelings are within your control. You can shift your focus, even if it doesn't feel like it right now. With practice, you'll learn to recognize this power and start to understand how old habits and emotions might have led to self-sabotage (giving away your power) and a feeling of being a victim (feeling powerless). It's crucial to see how these archetypes are playing out in your life. Don't be too hard on yourself if you have them. Everyone does, but you can't change them if you don't know they're there.

Moving up a layer of the left wheel to the Core Perception (CP), water types experience a lot of rejection. All people experience rejection, but to water types, this experience has a big impact, therefore seemingly occurs more and feels intensely painful. There are two reasons. One is that water types feel emotions more intensely than the other types, and water types reject themselves because of the core complex of unworthiness. Belief in unworthiness is further confirmed, leaving a feeling of hopelessness. Without hope – depression, being lost, and possibly victimized might appear as fate, leading to a sense of feeling alone and unloved. Your instinct template makes you perceive this. You might feel like a victim because you may feel powerless to change this "fate". I'm going to give you the information that you need to change it, forever. You are powerful.

Exercise 2:
Reflect on past rejections. What behaviors led to them? They'd likely share common traits. Write about them to observe the patterns. How afraid were you? What thoughts raced through your mind? Where can you change your thoughts and feelings? For instance, "I crave companionship. I just want someone to love me. Why is that so difficult?" Setting boundaries with yourself might shift your thinking to, "I'm comfortable being alone rather than accepting someone who doesn't value me." This mantra helps you create a new sense of self-worth.

Exercise 3:
No matter what your beliefs are about God/Spirit/Universe/Allah, Shiva, … as a human being, you have some kind of relationship with that archetype. Even if your position is to ignore it. What do you believe about God? What is God? What do you believe God thinks of you? What is God's responsibility to you? What is your responsibility to God? Note: The term God may have some preconceived notions for you. Replace it with whatever you want, such as spirit, universe, Allah, or whatever works for you.

The next water type layer of the model is the Shadow (SH) of neediness and withdrawal. Shadow is a Jungian term that means something you place into your personal unawareness, for safekeeping, until you are ready to become aware of it … if you become aware of it. You don't have to. It can stay there forever if you want it to. There may be some shadows that should stay there like your ability to murder. The ones that are causing you unhappiness are the ones that need to emerge, such as the ways in which you engage the victim and saboteur archetypes.

In Archedomi, the shadow (SH) is a behavioral response to the Core Complex (CC). Feeling unworthy and unlovable, water can present an instinctual need for someone to love you no matter what. Someone else loving you in spite of your many perceived flaws provides a seeming sense of value and redemption (water molecules have to bond with other molecules to become what they are meant to become). Neediness can be seen in some common behaviors such as calling your love object when you feel insecure about whether or not they love you, not allowing time or space for the relationship to develop, and driving by their place to see if they're home alone. A constant need for reassurance comes out in many behaviors. For example, I was once at a gathering and saw an old friend from high school. I was happy to see him and hugged him hello. I could feel his wife's insecurity. Sure enough, within a minute she asked if we had dated in high school. We had not, but it was utmost on her mind. She watched me very closely for the duration of the evening.

In large groups, you may stand alone on the sidelines (withdrawn), observing others. Through water perception, you only have a chance at acceptance if you find just the right person to see you. If a large group sees you, you believe that you might be rejected. You might think that someone will figure out that you're not worth having around. This is withdrawing behavior. If you allow yourself to withdraw from groups, it can feed your instinctive desire to only interact with one person at a time – that one molecule needed to become what you are meant to be, in your perception.

Exercise 4:
Think about how you might come across to others as needy or withdrawn. Write about it, or make a list. This exercise is most helpful when you can be honest with yourself. No one else has to see it.

Exercise 5:
How do you try to fit in with others? Water types often change their personalities to please others. They ask themselves, 'What do I have to do to make them love me?' Do you have to become a hiker, a swimmer, or something else? What have you done to change (shape) yourself to be what you think others want?

Reaching the outer layer of the left wheel, water types have an Addictive Response (AR) of connection through intensity. Water craves intense emotions to feel alive. You might see yourself as very loving and caring because you have strong loving emotions, but when seeing through the instinct lens, water uses emotion to reinforce negative patterns.

Water's preferred instinct way of connecting with others is through intense emotional pain. Emotional connection does not have to be intense or painful. It can happen through genuinely loving others. Genuine love is always given from a detached position. Giving love is what a healer does (the healer archetype belongs to the wholeness side of water). Detachment means you're connecting with others without any hidden motives or expectations. It's about setting healthy boundaries and being true to yourself. By practicing detachment, you can break free from this pattern and experience genuine, loving connections without pain or rejection.

Exercise 6:
Write about one situation in which you connected with one other through emotional pain. How did that experience make you feel good? How did it cause you to feel insecure? Did the connection last or did it dry up? How intense was it?

What are you passionate about giving to the world and how can you shift your focus to that?

Exercise 7:
Let's explore the various forms of love. Our language might not fully encompass them, but do your best to define them. For each type of love, can you tell me how much trust is required? You may want to use a scale of 1 to 10 to help illustrate this. Also, what kind of love are you seeking? Here are a few examples: romantic love, family love, sibling love, compassionate love, altruistic love, friendship, and inner peace.

Let's chat about boundaries for a bit. In some of the exercises, I'll ask you to think about them. What are they? Many of you understand that having boundaries means setting rules for how others should treat you. That's one way to do it. Another way is to hold yourself accountable for how you think, feel, and act regardless of what others are doing. Internal boundaries are super important for your well-being because they tell you how much you love yourself. If you have good inner boundaries, nothing outside of you can bother you. There are lots of ways to have inner boundaries, and that's where the real joy comes from.

Moving to the right wheel for water, the outer ring holds your Awareness Focus (AF) of boundaries through thought. Since water is highly emotional and lacks a distinct shape (boundaries), the water person's most effective tool is to step out of their emotional body and into their mental body to inquire about the necessity of boundaries in the present moment. Emotions are meant to serve as information rather than a permanent dwelling place. When you lack boundaries, both inner and outer, you may experience a familiar gut feeling or anxiety. This is your wisdom manifesting through your body, signaling that something is amiss. Something is about to occur where you lack trust in your ability to make the best decision for yourself. Something familiar is about to lead to another rejection. In this very moment, you have the opportunity to alter your experience and give yourself structure, akin to building your own bucket. Shift your thoughts. Instead of asking, "What can I do to make them love me?" reframe your question to, "What do they have to offer me?" In what way do I need to value myself (stop repeating old addictive behaviors that cause rejection) in this situation?

Exercise 8:
Reflect on the last time you faced rejection. How did you sense it was coming? What emotions stirred up before the familiar experience? Did you act out behaviors that scared you? Were there any actions that might have given you a hint?

The act of setting and holding firm to boundaries is how to build your own bucket, a container for your sense of self-value. Why does this work? Because as long as you shape yourself to what you think others want you to be, you are telling yourself that you have no value outside of them.

Truthfully, the only way to value yourself is to give yourself a container in which to exist. You don't have to accept crumbs of affection. You are supposed to reject someone who is not good for you. The hard part here is to understand that by accepting that which is not worth having, you are telling yourself that you are not worth loving. The truth is this: No one is obligated to love you. The only person who can make you feel valued is you. Now you can learn how to do that. No matter how hard you work to make someone else love you, it is not possible to accomplish. And others loving you won't make you feel more valued or more secure. Your task within the water pattern is to build self-value, and the only way to do that for you is to get good at defining boundaries, be good at rejecting that which is not worth having, and be willing to be alone rather than tolerate what does not work for you. Don't waste one more minute of your precious life on allowing yourself to be in pain. Boundaries create self-value.

Exercise 9:
Let's revisit the scenario from exercise 8. Now, imagine if you had set different boundaries. What might they have been? How would you have felt setting and maintaining them? And how would you feel about yourself, even if someone else got upset with you for standing up for yourself?

The next layer on the right wheel (from the outside in) is the Action Task (AT). For you, accepting your flaws is a significant milestone. This acceptance means you can stop criticizing yourself for not living up to unrealistic expectations. By acknowledging your flaws, you eliminate the constant worry that you aren't worthy of love and affection from those who care about you. Embracing self-love is what draws people towards you.

A red flag of non-acceptance is when you talk about what's wrong with you too soon in a relationship, especially if you carry negative feelings about it. Instead of waiting for people to reject you, you jump in and tell them why they should. Instead, focus on what's right with you. It's a good habit to have a list of positive qualities ready to go, or you can just answer their questions about you. If you're honest about your flaws, make sure you're fully accepting them before sharing too much too soon. Setting clear inner boundaries is important for healthy relationships.

Exercise 10:
Look closely at the ways in which you reject yourself. List out all of your flaws. Ask friends what they think your flaws are and give them a pass for telling you. Remain observant and non-defensive. You need to know this. Then go through the list. Which ones do others have? Are those who have them still acceptable people? If not, why not? Which flaws do you need/want to change? Form a plan for changing them. You have the power to do so if you wish. This process forces you to make your flaws emerge into awareness, then choose which ones to accept and which ones to change. You'll still have some, no matter what, so you don't have to worry about being too perfect.

There's an order to things. Water-type people must build trust in relationships or friendships before revealing flaws upfront. Allow time for relationships to build – at least a few months. You may need 3 months, or more, to know if someone will work for you or not. Then you become aware of the red flags. Immediate gratification does not work in relationships. If you want to build a long-term relationship, it has to develop over time, while accepting your own flaws. If others call you out on your flaws, so what? It's okay to have them. Accept them. For romantic relationships, if you want to build a long-term situation, do not have sex before you know that you love them, and that they love you. Sex is bonding and water types take it as a bond. It puts the situation out of order. First comes love, then marriage (marriage is a union like sex). If you don't want marriage, then it doesn't matter much. I'm not talking about legal marriage. Marriage is the mutual agreement to witness each other's life journey. This is an energetic marriage. Legal marriage is another matter.

Exercise 11:
In what ways have you historically entered relationships out of order? How have you built trust? Or did you just openly trust without others having to earn it? Who do you know who has a successful relationship? Can you ask them how they built trust? What does it look like to do that? Research it. Form a plan for the order of building a relationship. Meet, date, discuss the time needed to see if this is workable. Added note to this exercise: Water people like to give a relationship every possible chance to succeed. This often translates as giving a non-working relationship too much time. Water people are afraid that they will never find love, so they cling to every opportunity like glue. Be willing to reject it if it isn't working. You will get what you are willing to accept!! Three to six months is the most time you need to know the answer. I know that rejecting someone is the hardest thing you can imagine doing, but that is what is needed to value yourself when someone is not what you want.

The Positive Force of loving and nurturing, as well as the Gift of Grace of self-value, both occur naturally as side effects of working the AF and AT. You don't have to work at these two final attributes. When you value yourself, you become a healer of others. You help them with their emotional process and how to manage their emotions as information and self-containment. You become a giving healer without giving yourself away. And you love yourself doing it!

Fire

Fire, as an element, needs to burn and consume something to stay alive. It's like a little kid that needs to be watched and kept in check.
Containing fire is tough, and it's always hungry for more. The bigger it gets, the more it wants to eat, and the stronger it becomes. On a basic level, fire doesn't understand that a slower, gentler burn would be more respected. You can't help but be amazed by a fire, but a roaring, wild blaze can be scary and make you want to put it out.

> "A new commandment that I give unto you, that ye love one another; as I have loved you, that ye also love one another" (Yeshua, King James Bible. John 13:34).

Fire types struggle to find their identity because they lack a sense of self (like water). This emptiness makes it tough for them to look inward and understand themselves. Mirroring is a way for people to understand each other's perspectives. Our brains have mirror neurons that help us predict and project others' intentions and behaviors. This is how we become aware of ourselves and others, and it's the foundation of our relationships.

Please don't take these descriptors as harsh judgments. They sound unpleasant because they operate from fear and are described in their extreme negative state to make them clear.

The extreme negative archetype for the fire pattern is narcissism. Interestingly, narcissists seem to have either a lack of mirror neurons or dysfunctional ones.[10] People with the fire pattern can easily misinterpret situations, seeing attacks and betrayals where there aren't any. They might even twist reality to fit their perception of danger. If someone can't see things from another person's perspective, they naturally have less empathy and see them as a threat. It's not that fire needs to be mirrored, although they do, it's more about being open to mirroring others and really seeing them.

In Greek mythology, Narcissus was a man who was so enamored with his reflection that he couldn't look away. This obsession with his own image caused him immense pain and suffering. He eventually died of grief, realizing that true love seemed unreachable. When a fire type's perception remains in instinct, there may be an ongoing sense of grief. It is innate to a human being to seek higher self. Instinct is the opposite of that so remaining within its patterns of perception keeps one suffering with longing, grief, low self-esteem, and fear.

There is an interesting tool with mirroring, when the fire type is narcissistic, or simply in strong denial of its own perceptions. The I-Ching holds a concept called the "crescendo of awfulness".[11] It's a buildup of tension in the opposites, or tension in mirroring denied. When a strong fire type projects their interpretation onto others, villainizing them, correct mirroring does not happen. Instead, the fire perspective is projected onto others. What the other can do to create a correct mirror for the fire type is follow the I-Ching's advice to "hold still, hold firm, and hold together" meaning "keep inner thoughts quiet and neutral . . . do not doubt inner

[10] Goulston, M. (2010).
[11] Anthony, C. K. (1988). Hexagram 26.

sense of truth . . . [and] hold firm to what is correct". This means that when you practice mastery of remaining heart-centered, present, neutral, and non-reactive, the fire type has no choice but to see itself, like looking in a mirror. When you don't react in any negative way, the other has to see its own reflection. The tension builds to a point that is very difficult to hold, but if you can hold it, the fire type has no choice but to be the portal for the breakthrough, seeing itself. I've had to do this with people and it is not easy, but the results are amazing to experience. It allows the narcissist to breakthrough and self-reflect. And by the way, remaining non-reactive does NOT mean that you shouldn't have boundaries. Hold boundaries, but do so as heart-centeredly as possible.

Not all fire type people are narcissists, but I believe that all narcissists do fall under the fire type. The other types reflect through others, but fire has to find itself alone or through more limited mirroring. Mirroring is a psychological phenomenon that helps us blend in with our culture, family, or groups. Without the ability to mirror, one might always feel like an outsider, like a piece of the puzzle that doesn't quite fit.

Science knows that the brain has elasticity, creating new neural networks that accommodate experience.[12] This means that the more you intentionally work to change how you perceive, the more of the corrected neurons will be created. For fire, this means that if you actively work to see other people's point of view and exercise compassionate responses, the more you will move your perceptions to wholeness.

---

[12] Newhouse, E. (2012).

Milder fire types empower others and uplift them. The non-narcissist fire type brings joy, playfulness, and power to get things done. Milder forms still struggle with seeking material resources to excess, but they are more fun to have around.

Exercise 12:
How frequently do you experience anger or resentment towards others? In which situations do you feel like you belong? In which situations do you feel like a misfit? (Quantify these feelings by assigning percentages, for instance, determine the percentage of situations where you feel like you belong.) How do you compensate for the feelings of not belonging to enable you to exist in this world? In what ways have you experienced mirroring? What emotions do you experience when others fail to comprehend your perspective? How frequently does this occur?

Fire sees mostly its own point of view. Each type must move toward its opposite in positive ways to begin reuniting the elements into wholeness.

Sharing an axis of Self with water, fire types also deal with a sense of self, but they approach it differently. Where water feels unworthy, fire feels empty and non-existent, but compensates with an inflated sense of self. Water builds self-esteem through self-imposed boundaries, while fire builds the right to exist through humility. Fire types must experience rejection to gain humility and fill the emptiness with acceptance of flaws, of their humanity. This is the beginning of self as a human being. They need others to hold lines for them to experience humility. Their armor can be thick, so it's a task at times.

Exercise 13:
How are rejection and betrayal similar? How are they different? Give some examples of your experience with these? Have you wanted revenge for them? Give some examples of how you have rejected or betrayed others. No judgment. Everyone has done these things if you see it from other's perspective.

For fire types, the Core Perception (CP) is betrayal, which is a form of rejection because it might say to you that you're not valued enough to get what you want. Fire's instinct is to get what it wants because it's trying to fill the emptiness inside. Fire thinks not getting what it wants means it doesn't have the right to exist (this may be outside of awareness). What fire wants is endless resources. Not getting what you want for a while keeps that empty feeling inside, which makes you think you don't matter. But in the long run, not getting what you want helps you realize that you'll still exist even if you don't get what you want. You're not actually fire that needs to burn and consume to live. You're just a piece of God like everyone else. If you let your flame burn slowly like a candle, there'll always be enough for you. Keeping a bon fire going is much harder.

> "No man can serve two masters: for either he will hate the one, and love the other; or else he will hold to the one, and despise the other. Ye cannot serve God and mammon [riches]" (Yeshua, King James Bible. Matthew, 6:24). *The instinct side of fire derives from emptiness and seeks fullness through worldly riches. This pursuit perpetuates the emptiness.*

Exercise 14:
Consider writing about a time when you felt betrayed. What happened? What did the other do to betray you? What do you think was driving their betrayal? Were they trying to keep themselves alive too, or were they simply a cruel person?

The Shadow of denial (armor) is stronger in the fire type because it's protecting the psyche. Denial gives you the space and time to take a step back and reflect on yourself in a healthy way. If you try to see things too realistically too soon, you could hurt your psyche. In a way, denial is your ally. But it can also cause you problems if you don't grow or move your instincts into wholeness. It can slow you down too much. Only you can decide what you need. Your Shadow of denial is something to be aware of and accept as one of your flaws, but with a purpose, just like most flaws.

Exercise 15:
Have you ever felt like someone was criticizing you unfairly, and you couldn't believe they were right? It's common to dismiss such feedback, but it's important to take a step back and reconsider. Make a list of the things people have said, and ask yourself if there's any truth to them. If more than one person mentioned it, it might be worth taking their perspective seriously. If not, consider asking some trusted friends for their thoughts.

Fire, as an element, needs resources to survive. It must burn and consume to exist. This means that controlling resources becomes super important. The instinct lens of fire wants power to control assets, and if it appears to others as perfect, it can have more power over those assets. The Addictive Response (AR) for fire then is power and perfection.

Appearing perfect has another benefit of helping to thwart the emptiness as fire becomes its own mirror, but it does so in a way that is not the most helpful. Denial allows it to act as its own mirror, but limits growth or movement to the whole side of consciousness.

Exercise 16:
Think about some times when you wanted power just because you didn't trust others to have it. Now, pick two friends you feel comfortable with and ask them to share, if they're up for it, some ways you use power that might not be the best for you, and some ways that could be.

Moving to the right wheel to achieve wholeness allows fire types to begin the journey towards fulfillment (filling the emptiness) by practicing the act of seeing others' point of view. The Awareness Focus (AF) of seeing another's point of view helps you to self-reflect. This action builds your missing mirror, allowing your instinct lens of emptiness to be put aside and out of the way.

Exercise 17:
Have you considered things from their point of view? Imagine you're in their shoes and try to understand the situation. An exercise that may help is to use two chairs. Assign each one chair to you and one to the other person you are imagining talking to. Move back and forth between the chairs taking turns speaking as each person. Write down your thoughts from both sides. This will help you fill in the missing pieces.

Fire's Action Task (AT) is serving and giving to others. As it grows, it can transform into acts of service and giving to the world without feeling threatened. This natural inclination leads to the development of fire's Positive Force (PF), which yearns to empower others to shine brightly and radiate like stars in the sky. Subsequently, this nurturing force manifests as your Gift of Grace (GG): compassion.

To take your psyche from the instinct template of emptiness at birth to the compassion of a great leader who empowers others by giving them what they need without concern for what you get out of it is to bring your full agency into the world in an unforgettable way!

Exercise 18:
In what ways have you been of service to others? How do you envision yourself serving others in the future? Take action and document your experience. Consider making an anonymous donation or volunteering for a cause that, in the past, has intimidated you.

A final point about the fire type instinct perspective is that fire types tend to own most of the resources. Many elite and wealthy individuals belong to this type. Their desire not to rely on anyone for their survival leads them to believe that they have built their businesses solely on their own efforts. However, the truth is that others worked for them. Fire takes the lead and needs to perceive itself as a leader rather than an owner. It was the collective efforts of others that made resources available to them. Leadership requires a different psychological position than ownership. Leadership involves cooperation rather than competition, gratitude rather than authority. This is how one burns as a candle rather than an all-consuming blaze.

Earth

Sharing an axis of knowledge with air, earth types are imprinted with a Core Complex (CC) of chaos. A feeling of non-linear disorganization centers itself in the gut of this instinct imprint. Being on the axis of knowledge, information seems to come in random bits and pieces, without structure or form. The feeling of chaos might also be called anxiety or fear. It is an energy that has no place to rest other than in the pit of one's stomach as a constant companion, soothed only on occasion when a piece of the mysterious puzzle falls into place.

Exercise 19:

How do you store information? What is your process for learning a new topic? Do you take notes? Do you outline a book or presentation? How do you structure information as it comes in? Do you ever feel like you have all of the pieces? If so, under what circumstances?

Within the earth type imprint lies a direct consequence of chaos: the relentless drive to know everything, to find all the pieces of information that exist. Gaining new information gives order and meaning to the instinctual mind, but earth types live in the non-linear world of mysteries and beliefs. Belief systems serve as

> *The earth type seeks understanding of God and the Universe, the mysteries. It's task is to use that to become wise enough to remain silent allowing others know things too.* "Unto all riches of the full assurance of understanding, to the acknowledgement of the mystery of God, and of the Father, and of Christ; In whom are hid all the treasures of wisdom and knowledge" (King James Bible. Colossians 2:2-3).

coping mechanisms. The earth imprint might be the home of religion, spirituality, and philosophy because meaning and symbolism fill in the unknown. With the ever-present unknown occupying the psyche in this imprint, the Core Perception (CP) here is "Need to know," and this need is about God, the universe, the mysteries, and the void of awareness. It is here that belief systems, and their embedded coping mechanisms, are created.

Exercise 20:
On a scale of 1 to 10, with one being the least and 10 being the most, to what degree do you want to know everything? To what degree does it bother you to say, "I don't know"? What would happen if you didn't know something?

Earth type imprints have a Shadow (SH) behavior of control and stubbornness. If you control your environment and surroundings, you're never caught off guard by the chaos of the unknown. You are likely a homebody because you have more control at home than you do out in the world. If you venture out into the world, you find yourself at the same familiar gas station, grocery store, and restaurants, ordering the same food each time. This is all to avoid the unknown, which feels chaotic and activates your discomfort.

Exercise 21:
Think about the things you do over and over again. Then, make a list of new things you've tried. It's fine to enjoy your own company at home, watching TV and reading. But, how happy are you with your routine? What parts of it do you want to change? Make a plan to make those changes and take those steps! Ask friends for help. Don't have any friends? That may need to change.

Another part of the Earth shadow of control happens when you go out to gatherings of people. You may feel a need to share how much you know, to step into the teacher role. You may even see other people as peasants who would be much better off if they would just listen to you. In this way, you might come across to others as arrogant and self-important, a know-it-all, and find yourself an unwelcome guest, further isolating you. Sometimes, Earth types can be so attached to the idea of teaching what they know, and being the one who knows everything, that they will only have relationships with people who can be their "students". Consider how much this might be true for you.

Driven by the desire to comprehend God and the universe, the emergence of religion and spiritual practices are developed by the earth pattern. As one delves deeper into these beliefs, they can be instinctually concretized as righteous knowledge, fostering the growth of the ideal self. However, the instinctual mind, driven by survival, seeks to maintain ignorance of the spiritual realm. It convinces individuals that meeting their ideal self standards is an insurmountable task, an impossible feat. When we tell ourselves that something is too challenging to change, it is our instinct that keeps us separated from our ideal selves. It is not an insurmountable task; it is a choice. It is a choice to take responsibility for our ideals and either live them or accept that we have chosen not to.

When we fail to live up to our ideals, particularly religious ones, we tend to project them onto others, attempting to force them to conform to our ideals. This phenomenon was evident during the time of Yeshua, as exemplified by the Pharisees and Sadducees, who compelled everyone to adhere to their ideals of "God's laws" or the laws of Moses.

Exercise 22:
Look at how isolated you are and how isolated you want to be. If you want more friends, have you considered asking others what they know and listening to them without arguing a point or correcting them?

Earth types have an insatiable thirst for knowledge, constantly seeking more information. They often have a vast collection of books or a well-used library card, and their homes are filled with papers, all holding information they don't know what to do with. They might have moved away from physical storage and now keep everything electronically, but somehow, they still manage to collect more information than the other types. As an Earth person, you might find yourself constantly seeking information through workshops, classes, or other learning opportunities, like an information junkie. While seeking knowledge fills in the gaps of the unknown, structuring it or organizing it in a way that makes sense to you is driven by the chaos and the desire to make sense of it all.

Exercise 23:
How often do you take classes and workshops? How big is your library? How much paper do you have around your home? Does any of this bother you? Do you ever feel satisfied that you know enough? If so, under what circumstances does that happen? How much time passes before the anxious chaos of the unknown creeps back into your awareness as a need to seek again?

Gathering all of that information means that you do know a lot. However, no one likes to get advice they haven't asked for, or information they haven't asked for. The Awareness Focus (AF) for Earth suggests that being open to learning from others will help you realize that you don't need to know everything yourself. It's okay to trust others to know things that you do not. A good practice might be to ask others if they want information. Most of the time, people want support, not advice or solutions, at least at first. They know what they need. If not, they'll ask. Offer support first and ask what that means for them. Support may be different for everyone. Unsolicited advice does not hold others capable of knowing what they need for themselves.

Exercise 24:
How receptive are you to the knowledge and perspectives of others? Do you engage in arguments with them over specific points? Do you feel compelled to be right? If so, why is that? What does it imply when you are mistaken?

Earth is a realm of knowledge and exploration of the mysteries that lie beyond the physical realm. Your unique nature yearns to comprehend the profound mysteries of existence, particularly the nature of God and the Universe. Consequently, your Action Task (AT) lies in cultivating a profound sense of spiritual connection that grants you insight and a belief in something greater than yourself, a higher power that can guide and protect you without the need for constant control. By embracing this spiritual connection, you can trust that the divine will be privy to your thoughts and actions, allowing you to let go of the burden of knowing everything. Embrace the practice of listening to your inner voice of intuition, and allow it to guide you on an 'as needed' basis. Surrender to this practice, and you will find that you no longer need to possess complete knowledge.

A friendly reminder that your beliefs are meant to bring you comfort and well-being. They're like a safety net, not a weapon to judge others for having different ideas. Others' views don't pose any threat to you. If you start feeling threatened by them (it shows up as a desire to be right), it might be a sign that more letting go may be needed. Relying on instinctual (and not-so-true) beliefs to feel right, and using "God" as an excuse to feel in control, is not the way to go.

Exercise 25:
How do you currently surrender to God, your beliefs, or your inner wisdom? What ways can you imagine doing that? Here's a quick example you can try. When you cook something in the oven, don't set a timer. Instead, ask your higher self to let you know when it's done. Then, forget about it. When you suddenly have a thought that it's time to check, do so. It works! You can try this in other ways if you don't cook. Many people wake up without an alarm. Do that too. Chaos happens when we're disconnected from our higher selves. Tune into it.

Your Awareness Focus and Action Task naturally lead you to your Positive Force (PF) and Gift of Grace (GG), which are Discernment/Objectivity and Trust. While in the instinct mind, earth types can be judgmental of others. Judging them as not intelligent enough or knowledgeable enough allows you to feel in control of the knowledge. As long as you are the one who possesses the most knowledge, you feel secure and comfortable. Discernment gives you the chance to acknowledge that you are not omniscient and allow others to possess knowledge that you lack. This recognition can be a source of relief—the realization that you don't need to know everything. You know?

To be in a state of knowing guided by inner wisdom brings you back to the wise oracle archetype you are destined to embody. With practice, you have learned how to intuitively recognize that inner voice that possesses far more knowledge than you could ever comprehend. This realization brings a sense of relief. Part of this wisdom lies in understanding that the expression of knowledge is not always necessary. Allowing others to discover knowledge for themselves can be quite beneficial.

Exercise 26:

Can you think of a time when you didn't trust your inner wisdom to guide you? Describe what happened and how it turned out. Then, think of a time when you did trust your inner wisdom and listened to your gut. Share how that experience went. If you haven't had a chance to listen to your inner guidance, try the experiment suggested in exercise 25 and share your thoughts here.

> "O my father, if it be possible let this cup pass from me: nevertheless not as I will, but as thou wilt" (Yeshua, King James Bible. Matthew, 26:39). In his fear of the impending physical suffering, Yeshua then asked Peter, James and John to "watch and pray, that ye enter not into temptation: the spirit indeed is willing, but the flesh is weak" (King James Bible. Matthew, 26:41). *The temptation was great to exercise his instinct will over that of higher self who holds the bigger picture and mission in awareness. Allowing people to see the faith in this man who is willing to surrender to God (higher self), to his death, is what brought his message through the age. Earth types must surrender control to God and give up rigid beliefs.*

Air

As an element, air is perpetually in motion, entering and exiting every living entity. The air I breathe is the same air you breathe, and the same air that trees absorb to purify, returning it to the atmosphere for us to breathe. Connected to both the animal and plant kingdoms, air unites everything on the planet.

Taking your first breath, air entangles you to the instinct world, as though you have bitten from the apple that fell from the tree of knowledge of good and evil–setting the dichotomous dynamic in which you find yourself–separated from the tree of life: wholeness. In this way, air possesses a twofold existence. It separates and it connects. Taking the first breath separates you from wholeness. Releasing the last breath reconnects you to wholeness. BUT, you can reconnect to wholeness while still in the body. No need to pass first.

Sharing the axis of knowledge with Earth type, the element of Air represents secular, scientific kinds of knowledge governed by the mental body. While Earth seeks to unravel the mysteries of the universe, Air seeks logic and reason, providing explanations for the physical world. This element gave birth to the modern scientific method, which eschews emotions and intuition in favor of pure logic and objectivity. In this way, intellect separates soul and mind.

> "Which of you by taking thought can add one cubit to his stature" (Yeshua. King James Bible. Matthew 6:27)? *Here Yeshua refers to the seeking of positive validation from others. What others think of you is of no concern, positive or negative. This is also an air type position. Air people seek validation by taking on responsibility they shouldn't and putting others before themselves. They like to rescue others to some degree.*

In a seemingly different state, it also represents social

connections, and a desire for approval from others. Scientific knowledge connects everyone. The hard-won truths of how the world functions help everyone equally. That is how this element is one thing even though it seems like two things. Air is about connecting everything to everything through equality and social justice. Factual knowledge is a way to do that.

Air instinct imprints a Core Complex (CC) of fear of separation. As an air type, you likely have a strong aversion to anger and conflict because these experiences often lead to separation. For instance, you might say, "Why can't we all just get along?" or "Why do you have to yell? I hate yelling." To an air type, these actions are seen as forms of separation because anger itself is a means of separating people. While separation is sometimes necessary, it's difficult to comprehend when you're an air type. Air values connection above all else. Your greatest fear may be separation from others, which leaves you with a sense of abandonment or being left alone.

Exercise 27:
On a scale of 1 to 10 with 1 being not at all and 10 being absolutely, how much do you hate conflict? How much do you work to avoid it? What do you do to avoid it?

Because air belongs to the mental body, air types tend to have really fast minds, are smart, curious, and thoughtful. If this is you, you are kind and sweet. Most everyone likes you because you are so easy to get along with. Your strong mental body makes knowing how you feel a big challenge (Appendix B is a list of feeling words that may help). Consequently, your feelings often show up in your body as anxiety. Your fast mind, if not focused on something productive, turns to worry and angst. You might be the one who tells the kids not to climb the tree, or don't touch the hot stick. Your mind goes to the worst-case scenarios. The stronger your air type is, the more this happens.

When you don't know how you feel, you tend to put off your desires. Often, our wants and desires are connected to our emotions. Feelings help us figure out what really matters to us. Being unaware of your feelings makes it hard to know yourself and what you want. Because of your strong sense of responsibility and duty, the feelings you do experience are guilt, shame, and anger. Your Core Perception (CP) is then guilt and shame, the two feelings that you're most familiar with. I'd also add anger and resentment. Why? Your instinct mind wants to avoid conflict. To achieve this goal, you don't want to anger others, so you defer your wants. For example, someone asks you where you want to go for dinner. You say, "I don't care, wherever you want is fine," or "what movie do you want to see? "I don't care, whatever you want is fine." This avoids conflict, but it also prevents you from getting anything you want or need.

> "Can any one of you by worrying add a single hour to your life" (Yeshua. King James Bible. Matthew, 6:25)?
>
> "If you are in fear of the future, you're barely keeping up [immune system function] and the chemistry of your body is pressed upon . . . because you're afraid of life. Do you complain? This diminishes your life." (Kryon, Retrieved from: https://www.youtube.com/watch?v=oczYn6xMUwc, Loc. 13:50-14:36.

Not checking in with how you feel about something before making a decision is deference. Deferring to others all the time, eventually causes anger and resentment. Then you might blow up at the other person, creating conflict. As an air type, you might struggle to express your needs and feelings, which can lead to frustration when you don't get what you want. This cycle of guilt and shame can be tough to break.

Exercise 28:
How often do you know what you want and don't say it? What has been the typical result of that choice? What do you want the result to be?

The air imprint carries a Shadow(SH) of self-abandonment because every time you delay fulfilling your needs, you're essentially abandoning yourself. This behavior perpetuates your fear of being abandoned. Your imprint convinces you that others are constantly leaving you or will leave you, but in reality, you tend to leave yourself whenever you don't express your true feelings.

Exercise 29:
Think of the most recent situation in which you deferred to another. In that moment, your zeal to make them happy may have satisfied you. Now think about how it felt later on when you see them getting what they want while you, once again, go without. What is that like? How do you feel about it now?

Because air imprints upon you a fear of conflict, part of you is driven to make sure everyone else is happy at all times. Your Addictive Response (AR) to the fear of separation is to nurture others. Nurturing them helps to ensure that they are happy and will not leave you, abandon you, or separate from you. You also want the whole collective to stay connected so you may have designs on social activism or political support. Most air-type people do not want to be in the spotlight but rather be in a supportive role. This is another reason why everyone likes you. You are the server to many.

Exercise 30:
What does nurturing others mean to you? If you asked your friends and family in what ways they feel taken care of by you, what would they say? You can actually ask them if you wish. What do you believe about caring for others?

To begin moving the air instinct into wholeness, you can start with your Awareness Focus (AW) of setting boundaries through emotions by accessing how you feel about situations. When you are asked what you want for dinner, have an opinion. Your feelings are likely to be accessed through your body. Notice where you experience twinges. They can present as anxiety, nervousness, tension, or some other minor infraction on your peace. Positive feelings don't bother you, so you tend to feel those without issue. Any feelings of what you want that might create conflict are the ones that tend to be unconscious (in your body). An interesting trait of air types is that their unconscious emotions are sometimes picked up by those around them. I knew someone who would be telling a sad personal story, and everyone else in the room would be crying, while her eyes remained dry. I pointed this out to her, and she immediately owned it. From then on, she did her own crying. It isn't that you don't have feelings; you tend to push them away in favor of the mental body. That can change.

Exercise 31:
Can you imagine taking a strong position, or expressing a solid opinion, even when faced with someone being angry with you about your position? Describe what this would look

like, feel like, and possible outcomes in the aftermath. Name some positive outcomes here.

Setting boundaries with yourself is the first step toward your Action Task (AT) of embracing your inner sovereignty. Your personal authority needs to find a home within your belief system, your psyche, rather than living in your unawareness. Embracing your inner authority means that you always tell the truth even if it might upset the other person. But do it in a compassionate way so it is a mechanism for personal freedom from deferment. When you hold onto your wants and needs, and communicate them effectively and sympathetically, you have the power to become the great mediator you are meant to become. As a mediator, you act as an agent of God/higher self fulfilling your mission/purpose. You have the innate compassion to see all points of view and treat everyone with respect, equality, and fairness. When you can speak your truth with full authenticity, you are home.

Exercise 32:
What does inner sovereignty mean to you? How do you find the strength and will to hold an opinion in the face of someone getting angry with you for having it? What would it take for you to stop abandoning yourself by deferring your opinion to another? Having the courage to speak your truth provides your Positive Force (PF) as a natural side effect of utilizing your Action Task. Your Gift of Grace (GG) for the world, and yourself, is truth itself. You have no fear of expressing it when you step into your agency.

> "If ye continue in my word, then are ye my disciples indeed; and ye shall know the truth, and the truth shall make you free" (Yeshua. King James Bible. John, 8:31-32).

Part Three: Wholeness

> "Blessed are the pure in heart: for they shall see God" (Yeshua. King James Bible. Matthew, 5:8).

The opposite of instinct is wholeness, which is the higher self, or soul mind that is multidimensional. It sees everything all at once. Very few people have had access to wholeness, historically, but I believe that is about to change.

Wholeness is difficult to describe because that level of consciousness is communicated through image and feeling. Wholeness is love-based perceptions, a feeling of home, like none experienced before: a home that is filled with love, respect, support, compassion, listening, and full knowing of your true greatness of value.

How do you know that wholeness exists, that it's a real thing? You know because that constant and incessant longing for… something, is a promise built into your DNA. That longing drives you to seek… something. That something is home, truth, and wisdom from which you originate. Much like the waves of the ocean roll up onto shore bringing with them gifts of kelp, starfish, shells, sea-turtles, and more, they roll back out again to return those things to their origin. That is your incarnation. The promise of return home is built into the flow of life in the form of longing, much like a sea-turtle innately seeks the shore to continue its life cycle. You innately seek the thing that takes you home: God–in whatever term you want to use for it.

Part of the philosophy under which I operate is that wholeness is God. It has to be because wholeness is whole. It is the all of everything. Physics is beginning to show that the only thing to truly exist is consciousness, and it is an energy that permeates everything—one field. That is God, and therefore so are you. It is not possible for it to be any other way. I don't mean God as a personified being, but God as creation and consciousness itself. Incarnation shrouds your awareness, but that can change. You have access to your God-self, your higher self, your soul, or whatever you want to call it. For this reason, a spiritual practice is absolutely required to experience whole consciousness. You cannot avoid yourself. You cannot go home without taking you with you, and you are God.

Functions

Whole consciousness operates based on fundamental principles that I've structured into a system resembling a tree. The trunk represents the core of consciousness, with extensive branches that can further subdivide into numerous smaller branches, each harboring more nuanced concepts.

The trunk of wholeness could reach out into four branches of physical, emotional, mental, and spiritual. All four branches are part of every person. Because wholeness encompasses all four instinct patterns, the structure is not based on the elements. I said previously that physics understands that there is only one field of energy that is consciousness, so these four categories are really one, but categories allow for our linear minds to sort and process information. As Jung pointed out, a thing will remain unconscious, meaning outside of awareness, until it is seen or observed, and then it must be named to remain within awareness. If not named, it goes back into the chaotic soup of energy. For this reason, I sort and label the four planes to aid the linear mind with compartmentalizing this knowledge of self.

Becoming aware of what energy is doing in your life gives you the power to make choices about it. You have more control than you may realize. Your higher self communicates with you in many ways. I want you to know those ways, or at least what I can share with you in my limited capacity as an instinctual human being.

Wholeness is the opposite of instinct. Because instinct patterns of perception have dominated the human psyche, there is little frame of reference for how to be whole. New habits of mind must be formed, and that takes effort, patience, and acceptance of a process.

> *Higher self is always available and waiting for us to see it, but we have not been taught how to choose it.* Psalm 139:8 states, "If I ascend up into heaven, thou art there: If I make my bed in hell, behold, thou art there" (King James Bible).

You may have noticed that fire, which belongs to the spirit plane, has a core complex of emptiness. This might seem confusing. How can the home of spirit be empty? It's not spirit that's empty. Instinct is empty of spirit. Instinct is full of itself, which is the same thing as being empty of spirit.

Step one is to empty your instinct of itself, clearing it of self-concern. This is true for all types because wholeness is multi-dimensional. How do you empty your instinct? Fire offers a clue. It often experiences betrayal and grief. To empty your instinct, you need one act. This act will clear the heart center that connects higher and lower self. Keep in mind that the victim and saboteur archetypes are the most active within your instinct psyche. The one act that will clear your instinct and make room for your higher self is forgiveness. Forgive others for betraying you, abandoning you, rejecting you, confusing you, hurting you, not knowing how to be better, not knowing how to meet your ideal self, disappointing you and your sense of value or moral character, and not knowing how to be whole. Then, forgive yourself for also not knowing how to be whole, yet.

Forgiveness involves relinquishing the entitlement to be a victim. It entails releasing any feelings of anger, resentment, or bitterness towards another person. Forgiveness paves the way for compassion. It allows you to understand another person's perspective,

> "Forgive them for they know not what they do" (Yeshua, King James Bible. Luke, 23:34). *Yeshua cleared his heart before 'commending his soul to spirit'. He could not enter heaven (a state of being) without first clearing his instinct self, allowing heaven to enter into him.*

recognizing that they may have acted out of fear. Forgiveness doesn't mean tolerating bad behavior, having poor boundaries, or allowing someone back into your life who continues to hurt you. It simply means letting go of your fears (anger, resentment, victimhood, etc.) so that you can make room for higher awareness.

As you invite your higher self into your life, you'll notice that old feelings will surface into awareness, whether through dreams or wakeful states. People you haven't thought about in a long time, especially those who have hurt you, will occupy your thoughts, and you might wonder why. This is because your invitation to the higher self has opened those old wounds, giving you the opportunity to heal them. Only then can the higher self enter your awareness regularly.

Step two is awareness. The things to be aware of are:
- Your primary pattern, or whichever one you want to work on first.
- Keep in mind the Awareness Focus and Action Task for that pattern.
- The ways in which the victim archetype plays out within your patterns.
- The ways in which the saboteur archetype plays out within your patterns.
- Listening skills. Developing a relationship and open communication with your higher self. (Growing your intuitive skill is discussed in Part Four.)
- Self-esteem skills such as practicing inner independence, detachment, integrity to speak truth, see compassionately, and uplift others while discerning ideal and real selves.
- The four attributes of mastery provided by Kryon help you shift out of instinct.[13]
  - Remain heart-centered and present. If you are focused on the past or future, your instinct is running you.
  - Remain observant rather than reactive. What other people think or say is irrelevant to your truth.
  - Put joy in front of you. When you hold light (joy, peace, inner independence), darkness (instinct fears) cannot thrive around you.
  - Never diminish or lessen another person through judgment, gossip, or other negative perceptions.

Step three is acceptance of responsibility.
The instinct is addicted to negative fear-based patterns. It causes you to think and feel in ways that reduce its personal accountability. It prefers to place blame rather than allow for mistakes or imperfection. When you think things like, "I want to move into wholeness, but it's so hard." That is your

---
[13] Kryon. (April, 2024). Four Channellings on Mastery. Retrieved from: https://www.menus.kryon.com/hw-04-24-audios

instinct mind making you a victim of your own thought process. It makes excuses for the addictive behaviors to continue, like any addict who isn't ready to grow. And it's a form of sabotage. Moving awareness to wholeness is a moment-by-moment choice. You choose to move to heart-center and follow the mastery edicts listed above. That's it. Watch for instinct to play its game, then choose to take responsibility for your power and what happens to you.

Instinct also likes to make you take everything personally, as though your worth as a human being is on the line. If you relapse in developing new habits, and you will, you are NOT failing God or yourself. It is part of the process. Every relapse shows you that you want to dwell in wholeness because it feels better. Everyone has a CC, although everyone may have different things that activate their CC. When you make mistakes, your new mantra is, "So what!" You are imperfect. So what? You have an instinct. So what? You relapsed and started spiraling because you ran into an instinct activation. So what? You get the idea. Whatever it is, it does not speak to your value. Returning home to wholeness is the goal. Choose that rather than spend time and energy on self-deprecation. Choose to shift.

Step four is to be tested.
As you take your new habits into the world, you will be met with challenges that test your resolve. Water types will have to face acceptance of being alone in the world, in some way. This does not mean that you will be alone. It means that you have to accept your authority to become what you are meant to become, what you will give to the world. You must be willing to go alone as an independent person to accomplish that.

Fire types will have power and authority tested. You will have to learn how to share power and control, share resources with others, and recognize their need (compassion). Humility is the rule of the times.

Earth types must be open to learning from others, open to not knowing enough, open to being criticized for what you do know or proclaim. And willing to keep quiet while others express what they know. Don't be the rightest person in the room and don't treat every relationship as though you are the teacher and others the student.

Air types will be required to let people go, not to save everyone. Allow others to save themselves. It's great to help others, but when you do it at your personal expense, then it's a problem. You can be a workaholic because you want to rescue others. In the process, your instinct causes you to see only your goal of rescuing, and you might neglect those closest to you. If those you love feel like they don't matter to you, they will leave if they have any self-value at all. Balance what you give and allow others to help too.

Continue an ongoing resolve to maintain your new habits of mastery long enough to form a new neural network so your brain acts as a processor for wholeness rather than for instinct. Change happens, and it is good.

Part 4: Intuition

> "The comforter, which is the Holy Ghost, whom the Father will send in my name, he shall teach you all things, and bring all things to your remembrance, whatsoever I have said unto you" (King James Bible. John, 14:26). "I will not leave you comfortless. I will come to you" (John, 14:18). *Yeshua is your higher self because he is God embodied. So are you. That is how he comes to you. Yeshua had also said that his words would live forever. I believe he is saying that his words are God's words and because you are God, all things are always with you. You need only ask for that knowledge and wisdom to come to you and be open to it looking different than you may have expected.*

Intuition is how you connect to higher self. It can be used for everything you do every single day. The following is meant to get you started with some ideas of how to use it. This is by no means an exhaustive guide. You are a being of creation, and there exists a plethora of ways to use intuition and energy that you can create on your own. A good start is to ask for ideas to come to you. Invite them to come closer, to dwell with you.

Projection vs. Intuition

Projection is a Jungian idea that means to project onto another, much like a film image is projected onto a screen. When in a state of instinct consciousness, people project onto each other. Projection is the primary effect of instinct. Wholeness doesn't do that. For example, let's assume a water pattern is a person's instinct lens. The core complex of unworthiness will be projected onto others, and that can happen in a variety of ways. One example is if a man with a water pattern is raised by a man full of masculine machismo who is controlling or domineering and a mother who likes that kind of energy, the water-type male child will likely be soft-hearted and could project his low self-esteem as a result of his family dynamic around the machismo archetype. Especially if he is a large man, other men might challenge him for power, furthering his concept of not fitting in or not being enough because he is not macho. If this same water-patterned large man were raised by more feminine energy parents, he might project his low self-esteem (unworthiness) onto their softness, believing that he is soft because they are soft and maybe they did him a disservice. No matter what his parents were like, he is the same man with the same perception of himself due to his instinct pattern. Not due to his parents and their patterns.

Some things that you perceive or experience do affect your sense of self. Wider current culture believes that parents have to build their child's ego to keep them from suffering. It is true that being told how great you are or what is right with you empowers and builds you up. But your parents' behaviors are not the primary cause of instinct patterns. You were always going to see the world through your instinct lens. Some of that perception is projection. In fact, a large part of it is so.

When working with your intuition, how do you know when you are correctly perceiving information from your higher self and when you are projecting your ego/instinct's desires onto the situation? Experience is the primary way, but until you get more of that, what may be most helpful is to make sure that you are in a proper neutral state of mind when using your intuition, which I discuss next.

Communications: Preparation

Presence and Gratitude:
Being fully present in the now moment allows your awareness to focus in a peaceful, whole way. Insist on your thoughts staying on this moment, one at a time. What state of being gives you

> "Take the time to give prayers of gratitude that you are part of all of this beauty. See yourself reflected in it—for you are the grandest of all creations" (Kalei'iliahi, 2016, p. 48).

the most presence? Gratitude is a primary language for the multidimensional realm of wholeness, where your higher self resides. I don't mean to just say thank you. Images and feelings are the language of spirit. Feeling gratitude is necessary for your intuitive communications. Visualize what you are grateful for, and do so as often as possible. Gratitude releases you of your fear-based instinct. Whenever you feel fears on all levels from mild to extreme, you can step into gratitude and find peace. Sometimes, you may need help getting into gratitude. One thing you can do is make a short list of what you are grateful for. My list is my wife, kids, friends, nature, good health, a warm safe place to live, meaningful work, opportunities to help others, my dogs, etc. My list is long. I hope that yours is too. If you can't think of anything, the first item could be your life. You are here contributing your energy to the collective. You are loved and needed. You have a purpose, even if you're not clear what that is yet.

Gratitude is felt in the heart-center, where love is also felt. At any moment, you can shift your awareness to your heart-center. To find your heart center, place your index finger where your two collar bones meet at the base of your throat. Then four finger widths down and two inches inside your

chest. Place your awareness there in that spot. That is your heart-center. It is usually a place of peace. If not, try some of the following: (I'll add which element is used)
- (Water) Take a hot bath.
- (Water) Watch the current of a river, or the waves of a lake or ocean.
- (Earth) Spend time in nature, hug a tree.
- (Earth) Sometimes anger is due to lack of physical movement. Perhaps go for a walk, or do some yoga. If unable to move, visualize yourself moving.
- (Air) Breath work. There are many kinds of breath work. You might want to do some research on which types may appeal to you.
- (Air) Listen to meditative music. Listen to birds.
- (Fire) Gazing into a fire or candle.
- (Fire) Spend time in the bright sunshine.

Keep in mind that the element you need may be the opposite of the element that is struggling. This is because imbalances create tension and conflict. For example, if you are struggling with anger about not getting what you want (a fire attribute), you may need a water solution. Also, gratitude practice is a great way to get past anger. Even if all you are grateful for is having clean sheets, or food, or a cardboard box to cover you from the rain. There is always something to be grateful for. Focus on that.

Meditations
A daily practice of meditation has many health benefits and it also helps you prepare for communications with your higher self. Meditation empties your mind of the mundane world's clatter. It centers you, balances you by returning your awareness to your internal world of quiet.

Some useful meditation tools might be music, scents, sounds, spaces, and locations that, when you make them part of your daily practice regimen, automatically send you to your inner realm, readying you for connection. A habitual spark can ignite your connecting process much faster. I recommend that you choose sounds, sights, and smells that you have control over. I once wanted to track my dreams, so I trained myself to fall asleep to the sound of loud exhales out of my nose. This put me to sleep within a minute so I could be awakened by an alarm at the appropriate point in the sleep cycle. The problem came when I was sitting in a classroom, and the man behind me was breathing loudly through his nose. The sound prompted me to sleep. My head was bobbing up and down, and my eyes rolled up as I struggled profoundly to stay awake. Lesson learned.

Communications: To and From Higher Self

Ask the right questions.
With practice, you'll get good at asking the right questions, or asking in different ways because the higher self wants to be very clear with you. Its perception has no limits like yours does; therefore, it must take care how it answers you. I'll give an example. Often when doing medical intuitive work, I am asked to discern which supplements (herbs or vitamins) are the best option for people. I use an imaginal meter in my mind that has a needle that moves from 0 to 100 percent. I don't recall how we came to use a meter this way, but I tend to like quantitative answers when I can get them. It allows me to be clear with people. I've asked the higher self at what point a supplement is recommended, and the answer is 60 percent is acceptable. 80 percent or higher is best (I did not discern that with my instinct. I asked for that determination from the higher self.) Sometimes, the needle will bounce back and forth on the "meter". This means that one of the

variables of the question needs adjustment. It could be the dosage, how often it's taken, the duration it's taken, or something else. But the first step is to ask, "To what degree is this supplement beneficial for this person"? My state is neutral. I cannot have any bias about the supplement. It is not my place to judge it or the person taking it. What's good for me may not be good for them, and vice versa. Once it is determined that the supplement is 60 percent or better (and I prefer 80), then I can start asking more detailed questions like how many per day? Each day? If not, every other day? Every three days? and so on until my meter needle settles into a fixed position. I would also ask for how long this is a valid dosage because it could be that the person needs it for a couple of weeks and then needs to change the dosage? It is typical for the body to need change rather than a simple yes or no (two-dimensional) solution.[14]

The same is true on the emotional, mental, and spiritual planes. Sometimes you need more time with your emotions than other times, and so on. This is why intuitive communication is so important. Routines are nice, but not always right for you.

Trusting the Answers
Asking the right questions is substantive to obtaining good information, and trusting the answers is the next step in learning how to use your intuition. It takes time and experience to learn how true information feels. Information will be true when you keep your instinct/ego out of the situation through methods discussed above. Learning that you are NOT projecting your personal beliefs, ideas, expectations, and desires into your "listening" takes time.

---
[14] I would never do this with prescribed medication unless working with a physician. I am not a medical doctor.

Give yourself the grace to learn the difference between projection and intuition. And, if you are heart-centered, grateful for the information coming to you, and neutral in your biases, then it is very likely that you can trust what is coming through to you.

What is also true is that the more you know and study of our intellectual world, the easier it is for the higher self to communicate with you because you provide a library of choices for the higher self. It knows so much more than you do, or possibly ever will, that the more you do know, the easier you make its job of answering your questions. For example, if I wanted to work on helping people with only their physical problems, I might have studied to become a medical doctor so that I could use my medical intuitive skills much more effectively. However, I believe that consciousness matters more, so I chose to study psychology to help people on the soul level rather than the physical level. If your mind is functioning alongside spirit, your body likely will too. For this reason, I don't do many medical intuitive readings anymore. I focus on the psyche. Learning Jungian psychology gave me a foundational language and theory from which to develop my intuitive work.

You may notice that you feel called to read something, or learn something, only to discover that someone you talk to a few days later is in need of that information. This is one way in which you following your intuition to learn something serves you and others. You are given an opportunity to act as a conduit for others. That is one way a collective society works. Ongoing study is important to a life of whole consciousness, and it helps to connect you to the spiritual realm of the higher self. The more you know, the more you can trust what comes to you simply because you create a field of knowledge with which the higher self can reach you. Study is not limited to STEM-type pursuits. Arts are closely related to intuitive development. For now, you still have to study how to draw, or write, or whatever craft you take up. Studying develops your skill and therefore your access to the higher self. Creative acts always come from the unconscious realm. Problem-solving is a creative act, so the more you know, the easier it is to find solutions.

Imaginal Tools
Imaginal tools are like the meter I discussed previously. Because higher self knows way more than you do there is no limit to what tools you can create. Whatever it is, the higher self will understand it. In fact, the higher self is likely showing you the tool to use. I'll give some examples.

One idea is to ask for a symbol that means something. Let's say that you were raised by a person who displayed narcissistic behaviors. You have an instinct pattern of water, and you projected your unworthiness onto that person, trying desperately to get them to see you and love you. This might encourage your attraction to people who display narcissistic behaviors (your instinct pattern is still working to make another love you). You decide that you want to change your attraction to narcissistic people. You want to stop inviting that behavior into your life, but you have trouble seeing it clearly early on because your attraction to them feels magical (water). You see the behavior much too late. You can go into an intuitive position and ask your higher self for a symbol that represents a person who has narcissistic behaviors. Your higher self will show you a symbol. They are often humorous, so they might show you an image of Narcissus looking in a mirror. Let's just say that's what they did. You form an agreement with your higher self that when you meet someone that you are attracted to who has those behaviors, the symbol is presented within your mind's eye. This is your warning to stay away and look elsewhere, or plan on managing the relationship in a specific way. You could also form an agreement that with everyone you meet, you become aware of the symbol, and it will rotate one direction to show that the person is safe for you and the opposite direction to show that they are not safe for you. Or maybe they look in the mirror when they have those behaviors and away from it when they don't. You can create any type of communication device that you wish. Your higher self will honor it. Your higher self loves it when it can work with you. That is all it wants to do, to love you in this way. Ask it for guidance to show you what you need to understand.

Some people struggle with visual insight or images. Using sounds, smells, or any sense as an intuitive receiver is quite doable. You might feel sensations in your body. Try several ways to see what might work for you. Following are some more ways of communicating with higher self.

Sudden Thoughts, Feelings, or Visions
Another tool example might be to ask for a reminder thought. I do this all the time when cooking. I may have mentioned this one earlier. I ask my Higher Self to let me know when my food is done cooking. I find that using timers both weakens my intuitive skill and also mechanizes the cooking process, which, in my view, lessens the quality of the food. Using intuition in this way is like magic. I ask for the reminder and walk away. I can completely focus on something else. By not thinking about the food or constantly wondering if it's done, the sudden thought that I have to check it is perfectly timed. The sudden thought of "oh. Food

needs to come out" makes it turn out perfect every time. I never have to worry about it burning or being undercooked.

The reminder tool is also useful when I have to be someplace. I dislike having to pay attention to a clock or guessing how traffic is and how I might need to compensate. It's so much easier to just ask Higher Self to let me know when it's time to go. I ask it to provide enough time to get my coat on and use the bathroom or whatever. I always, always, arrive at my destination at the exact right time when I do this. No timers and no need to unnecessarily pull my attention away from what I'm doing.

Another communication that I can put into this category, that many of you already use, is asking to be woken up at a certain time. Kryon offered a great addition to this, which is to add that you want to wake up feeling fully rested, as though you've had a full eight hours of sleep, and your body chemically balanced. This is especially useful if you had to stay up late. What else can you think of to do with your intuitive communications?

Archetypes and Symbols/Images
Archetype is a term that Jung revived from Plato. It is from Greek terms Arche (Ark-ah) that means ancient or original, and Typos (tīpōs) which means blow or imprint. Jung described the archetype as a structuring pattern from the collective unconscious. Those patterns that belong to all people and emerge into awareness such as leader, time, mother, father, etc. Anything that every person would experience regardless of where they are from.

Your Higher Self might use archetypes or symbolism to communicate messages to you. For example, if you are out hiking and a snake crosses your path, you could ignore that and think nothing of it, or you could reflect on the possibility that it is symbolic of something. Snakes shed their skin, they transform themselves as they grow. They are capable of stealth. Snakes can loosen their jaw to consume food.[15] What might all of that mean for you? Personal transformation is either occurring, is about to occur, or needs to be allowed to occur. Only you can interpret this archetypal figure. I know that when I see a coyote, I think, "oh oh". Coyote is the trickster. If Higher Self can't get my attention another way, it will do something unexpected to get it.

When you begin to notice archetypal symbolism, your Higher Self is given a much larger menu of options for sending you messages. Archetypal symbolism can occur through animals, people and their behavior, weather, time and numbers, and everything else. Everything is a structured pattern of energy, or consciousness, which is why it can so easily be utilized for symbolic interpretation.

Sometimes symbolism comes through an accident. If you're unaware of something that you really need to be aware of, you may have an accident that gets your attention. It can be extreme, or it can be mild. Astrology can play a role in accidents too in that certain alignments can make you more vulnerable to accidents by virtue of timing. I once was driving down the freeway and entered a "zone" that felt like great potential for an accident. I gripped the steering wheel tightly and began checking all mirrors. A moment later, as I passed through the feeling, I saw in my rearview mirror, a small car zip across five lanes of traffic clipping the front bumper of the farthest vehicle. Both went spinning out of control. Fortunately, no one was hurt and the situation was

---

[15] Andrews, T. (2002, 2010).

not meant for me. But perhaps feeling that energy made me aware enough to keep me from changing lanes in that moment, to keep me from getting involved? Either way, it is always good to pay attention to energy and the events surrounding it. I can also look at the symbolism of being the one to successfully avoid an accident because I was paying attention. I like that lesson.

Synchronicity

Synchronicity[16] means experiencing a meaningful connection between the "psychic and material world" through acausal means.[17] An example I gave previously was of a snake crossing your path. Is this mere coincidence, or might it reflect an unconscious activity within your psyche? That is for you to decide. If you don't consider it a possibility, then you might not catch the message, if there is one. For a synchronicity to occur, it requires that you extract meaning from whatever is taking place.

To offer another example of synchronicity, if I've been thinking about someone I haven't talked to in a while, and this happens in a recurring manner over a few days, I've learned to interpret that as I need to call them. Something is up and either they need my help, or I need theirs. Every time I've called, it turns out to be the right thing to do. Something was indeed up.

The psychic contents often emerge into the physical, material world when one is unaware of inner feelings, or trying to suppress them as in the example I gave previously of my client's van being hit during the night. Another example is a woman who was very scared for her grandson

---

[16] Jung, C. G. (1981).
[17] Samuels, A. et. al. (2003).

because he was in some legal trouble. Her house (an archetypal image of the soul) had repeated issues with plumbing (water: emotions). Toilets broke, the house flooded, pipes burst, etc. Quantum physics is beginning to see that energy connects everything. That woman was not aware of externalized symbolism so she had a few more plumbing problems before the situation resolved, which was when her grandson avoided a long-term prison sentence. He managed a short-term stay in a juvenile detention facility. This was emotionally manageable to his grandmother.

Synchronicity is one of the easiest methods to utilize that allows you to begin shifting your awareness to your intuitive process. Communications from Higher Self often occur in this way simply because it's the most readily available. A car accident may not be a simple matter of an accident. Running into a friend may not be a coincidence. They might have a message for you. Always ask how things are going and if you can do anything for them. You may discover something about yourself in the process. And there are other ways synchronistic communications can manifest too.

Dreams
Dreams present you with feelings and images, the language of spirit, or the unconscious realm. They provide messages for your awareness whether the message is about a new idea emerging for you, or some unaware need you might have. Dream images can present shadows in many ways. Shadows being psychic contents that you are not aware of. Water is an image of the unconscious itself. It is the depth of the unknown (ocean), or emotions gone awry (raging river), or something similar. A dream in which you are on a boat looking into the depths of the ocean would be interpreted on how you are feeling about looking there. Are you afraid of

those depths? Are you soothed by them? If afraid, there may be something that you're unaware of that needs to be seen. If soothed, perhaps you've already seen what is in there and it brought relief. Do you dive in? If so, what do you see? What is it symbolically related to in your current life?

Dreams also bring new ideas that help steer you on your best path. This often happens to me in the form of waking up to some new idea or concept that I hadn't considered. It's a great way to problem-solve. Before going to sleep, ask Higher Self to send an idea that will help you find the direction that you need. Keep in mind, it may be a direction that is uncomfortable for you. Be grateful for the information, no matter what it is. It is also good to feel grateful when asking. Gratitude sets up the best energy dynamic for true and accurate information. Fear, anger, or resentment will cause you to create energies that may not be so pleasant.

Numbers

Ah, numbers! I love numbers. They are simple, uncomplicated symbols to find your way through your life. When you start seeing triple digits, that's just the best. These are small validations that you are thinking correctly and taking yourself through your journey in a valid way. 111 is a new beginning. 222 is taking the next step. Clock numbers are also a great way to receive validations that you're on the right track. 12:12, 11:11, 10:10, waking up at 3:33 or 4:44. Seeing a license plate with 777, or 888, or wherever your attention is suddenly drawn. Others, who are more knowledgeable than I, have already provided a great deal of information on numerology, so I won't do that here. It is a subject that deserves more attention than I can provide as an amateur numerologist.

Understanding the archetypal energy of numbers is a wonderful communication tool. Many years ago now, I was reading about numerology and a process that numerologists use called rooting down the number. Rooting means to make any number a single digit by adding the digits together. For example, 12 becomes 1 + 2 = 3. 248 becomes 2 + 4 + 8 = 14, then 1 + 4 = 5 so 248 is a 5. I finished reading that when I felt compelled to pick up a composition notebook and open the back cover. There I found a standard multiplication table. I began rooting down the numbers in my mind. I was seeing something in the table but I couldn't track the complexity so I drew out a table grid and began placing rooted down digits within it. What I saw, I called the Enneagrid (unrelated to the Enneagram). That is available to you in Appendix C. It led me to the concept of four as wholeness and this happened just about the same time I was receiving information on the four element instinct patterns.

Illness/physical or emotional changes

Working as a medical intuitive, it was common to see illness in people that resulted from years of thought patterns that block life force energy. Moods live in the body. Your chakras run energy in categorical systems.[18] When you are not practicing awareness of what you think or feel, problems show up physically. I've seen a few people who avoid, or ignore, their fated path or work for this life. Doing so usually leads to a catastrophic illness of some kind because that gets your attention. That sends you to God where you ask for help, where you finally invite your Higher Self into your life. If stepping into authority and responsibility is uncomfortable, it may be a sign that part of you is still functioning through instinct. Lean into your relationship with higher self and utilize the tools you are learning to

---
[18] Myss, C. (1996).

move into wholeness. Some ways in which your energy flow might get stopped up are in the following examples.

The root chakra, located at the base of your spine, is about your security and tribal connections. An example of this is one man who was approaching retirement and wondered why his lower back was hurting so much. He felt insecure about his financial prospects if he retired. Any kind of insecurity can influence this area. Chronic Fatigue Syndrome typically results from years of giving away life-force through constant deference. The mindset of needing to care for others or bow to others' control sends the message that you don't matter. The root chakra has a cord that runs into the earth. It absorbs the earth connection and nourishes your life. If you don't value your life, that cord shrivels up and can't process the life-giving energy that you need to thrive. That is Chronic Fatigue Syndrome, at least what I have seen of it.

The sacral chakra, located just below the belly button, is about sexual and creative energy. Any negative thinking about this area shows up here. One example I give of myself is that for so many years I absolutely hated my monthly cycle. I didn't like feeling horrible. I didn't like the mess of bleeding and the embarrassing occasions of not knowing when it would start. Over the years, I developed a uterus four times normal size due to fibroids. I had been sickly for years because of it.

Third up from the bottom is the solar plexus chakra, located just below your ribs at the center. This one is your ego/instinct, or sense of self. If you feel your energy in this area, it's likely about your sense of self within the instinct side of your psyche. If you have low self-esteem, it plays out here, affecting all abdominal organs and functions.

Fourth up the line is the heart chakra. This one is where I ask people to focus their awareness at the heart center. It is here that you can find peace. However, if you are thinking from your instinct in ways that don't allow love to process, then you might have difficulties here. I know one man who struggled to let love in. He didn't trust it. He developed lung cancer just to the left side of his heart, the receiving side.

Your fifth chakra is the throat and is located at the base, where your thyroid is. Each chakra is run by glands. I previously gave you an example of a throat chakra issue given that this one is about your will or volition. I shared previously about the woman who believed that she never got to do what she wanted. She developed a thyroid disease. Sixth/seventh up the line is the brow and crown chakras that control your ability to see beyond this world. They connect to your pineal gland and provide your insight or intuition. These two don't hold a lot of awareness for most people as of yet. That will change.

What you think matters. It matters a lot. Gratitude, love, joy, and peace are the cornerstones of good health. Period. And you have the power to choose. Keep in mind that when you feel powerless, that is the victim archetype ushering from your instinct. When that happens, tell yourself, "So what?" and adopt the power to choose in this moment.

Knowledge: Filters of information flow
Your Higher Self wants to help you. It wants to communicate with you, but it will absolutely allow you to choose it. Where instinct is loud and clamoring for your attention, Higher Self is quiet, still, and waiting for an invitation. It stands outside your door hoping that you'll open it to say hi. It waits patiently to say, "You are loved. How can I help you?"

Studying to gain knowledge can help your higher self communicate with you. If you don't know about physics, it probably can't lead you to the secrets of the universe (I don't know much about physics either). Einstein and Tesla both commented on the necessary use of intuition for guidance in their work. When I saw the connections between thoughts, feelings, and physical health, I needed a language for it, so I studied psychology. My Higher Self couldn't lead me very well into my work, my life's path, if I didn't have language and knowledge for it to use as communication tools. The more you know, the easier it is to find your way. Higher Self can't give you messages and hints about how to build a bridge if you don't even know what tools and materials are available to build it. Study your craft, whatever it is that you're passionate about. This is a benefit of being a lifelong learner. My passion is soul evolution, returning home to spirit. I study it. I work with it through intuition and energy. It's my thing.

Energy Work

Energy can be a mysterious and broad idea. It's a vibe, a feeling, a sound, an idea: it's consciousness, as well as the unconscious. Energy is everywhere and everything. It means frequency and vibration. On any given spectrum of labels or ideas, energy denotes a sense of reality beyond the physical and tangible realm. It is all the things we know to be real that can't be seen or touched, such as love, wind, gravity, magnetism, and time. Energy is multi-dimensional constructs that we accept as true, even though they are little understood. The one word, love, does not begin to express all the forms of love or the intensities of love. English needs a lot more words to explain just that one energetic experience.

Energy is part of being human. You have an energy system. The universe has an energy system, and both are that same system. At least I think so. I also think and experience energy as a way to heal, alter, create, and shield. Working energy is as straightforward as learning to think differently. It's a part of you. You have more ability to use it than you might realize.

As a side note, there is no physical limitation to energy. It does not matter if someone is sitting in the room with me or across the ocean from me. Energy is multi-dimensional, which means that it is perceived through the one field that is everywhere. Your awareness can focus in on a small part of it from anywhere. There is also no time limitation. I once had someone ask me to look at why she had trouble taking medications. They seemed to have the reverse effect for her. She said, "I'm good today, but I wish you could've seen me last Thursday." I said, "OK. I'll look at you last Thursday". Do not accept the premise that time is a limitation. It isn't. By the way, she was a rare person who had an inverted energy system.

Feeling energy with your hands
A simple exercise to shift your awareness to energy:
1. Rub your hands together. While you do so, pay attention to how your palms feel. You might notice that your skin tingles or experiences the sensation of friction.
2. Stop rubbing your hands together but do keep your attention on your palms and how they feel.
3. Hold your two hands a few inches apart while facing each other.
4. Begin to slowly and gently push and pull your hands toward and away from each other. Notice if you feel anything in your hands.

That is you feeling your own energy within your palm chakras. Hand energy portals are commonly used for sending and receiving energy in various forms, mostly for healing. Experiment with placing your awareness on your palms and inviting your Higher Self to send energy/information through your hands. Maybe this is your avenue? Maybe another works better for you. Try them all and then create some of your own, or ask your Higher Self to show you a way that works for you.

Feeling energy with your emotions
Many times when I've been conveying information or working an energy circle for others, I could feel emotion in the room. Sometimes it's anger, sometimes grief, rarely is it joy because most people don't seek the help of an energy worker if they are joyful. A most common occurrence is when I give a presentation on the Archedomi model. The water types are often in tears as I talk about their pattern and how they perpetuate their own pain. Their emotional grief and relief fills the room. Air types have difficulty feeling and they often project those emotions. Others then do the crying. If you feel emotions that seem out of place, ask that any emotions that do not belong to you be returned to their rightful person. If they stay with you, then they are yours. You could also put up a shield to stop them coming through you if they are not yours.

Feeling energy with your body
Some people need to invite energy into their body to understand and interpret it. I would use this as a last resort and only if I were experienced at how to neutralize it within myself. Inviting someone else's energy into your body is risky, to say the least. If I ran into this myself, I might tell the

person that I can't help them. If I can't understand what it is without bringing it into me, then I think I'll let it go. You can make a choice for yourself that feels comfortable for you. Having said that, most of the information I've written here is for you to work on yourself. Not for you to go around looking at and imposing yourself on others. That is not ethical. Please be kind and respectful of people's right to privacy and choice. Some things you may not be able to help seeing, but then you keep it to yourself.

Energy can also cause some anxiety. This is a way for the body to interpret that something you are unaware of may need your attention. This is common for air types that struggle to feel their emotions. Emotions guide our decision-making, and if you can't feel them, your emotions might present as physical anxiety. This is true for all types, as there are times for everyone when unawareness is the preferred safety mechanism. Anxiety is worth looking deeper into.

Seeing energy with your eyes
There are different ways to see energy. Some people can see it as if it were physically present. They can see its color and shape with full awareness. If this is your way of seeing energy, you will see auras when you are with people. You likely are aware of what the various colors and hues of color mean about a person. You see them as soft green feeling their openness and a balanced system, or you see them as red feeling their strong connection to physicality. Your experience of others tells you which colors belong to which meanings. To be clear, I don't see this way, so I have no experience of what colors mean.

Seeing energy like a memory
Some people, like myself, see energy with the eyes, but not in a physical way. I mean I don't see it like it's actually there. I see it like it's a memory, even though I know that I am seeing it right now. It's as if some part of my psyche is able to perceive it, but not the same way as if I'm seeing an object. Energy is non-physical. My eyes are seeing it in a multi-dimensional way, the same way that I hold a memory. It's exactly the same experience, in terms of visualization. I can feel that the time is present, not in the past. Sometimes, I can discern color, but mostly not. For me, I "see" energy in terms of meaning. I can feel it, like I feel personalities in people. I can look at someone and "see" that they have a headache, if I'm paying attention to how they feel. If I'm not paying attention, I may not notice that they have a headache. Why is this? Because there is so much happening all the time, in terms of energy, that no one can possibly place their awareness on everything all the time. It's too much for the two-dimensional instinct mind to manage. Energy is all about where you place your awareness, what you choose to be aware of.

Seeing energy with imagination
Seeing energy with imagination is different than perceiving it like a memory. Both ways involve imaging (recall that the language of spirit [energy] is feeling and image), but imagination comes into play when sending or working energy, not when receiving it in the form of information processing. Seeing energy with imagination is a way of sending energy. It is a creative process and that is very different from accepting it as a communication.

Sending energy

Whenever you actively work with energy, which is all the time, you are sending it somewhere to some effect, whether it's to others or to yourself. That effect can be positive or negative. I've discussed how the instinct mind produces fear-based negative thoughts and feelings. Those thoughts and feelings create energy, or block the flow of life-force energy. That has a definite effect upon your health and well-being. What you think and feel matters, very much.

Gratitude and love go a long way to preventing disease. Even the most fit and healthy eaters can get disease if their mind is not in cooperation with their ideals. It is human nature to possess inner conflicts due to the two-dimensional instinct way of being. That can change.

Sending energy with permission

If you send energy to another person, please make sure that it is love. If you feel anger or resentment toward them, neutralize it as quickly as possible and then send them love. You can always appreciate what they are showing you, even if you don't like it. When you intentionally send energy to another person, or being of any kind, ask permission first through the planes. What I mean is ask your Higher Self if it is okay, and their Higher Self, if you do that work. Sometimes, it may not be in your, or their, best interest. You can't know what Higher Self knows. What you do, even if well-intentioned, may have a negative effect on their mission, or path. For example, you may value living a long life and therefore want to send healing energy to a person dying of cancer. They may also want to be healed of cancer, but it may be that their Higher Self is preparing them to go home so they can come back to do a different task. You can't know that. You need to ask, always because human instinct understanding is very different than higher understanding. One tool you can use for this is the imaginal meter I mentioned previously. The question is, "To what degree is it beneficial for me to _____?" The meter can show you.

Sending energy with feelings and images
As I've said, the language of spirit (multi-dimensionalism) is feelings and images. When you send or create energy, you can utilize your imagination. Working energy with intention is a creative act and therefore requires some kind of vision accompanied by a feeling. There was a time when I really wanted to play the piano. I go through phases of musical ideation like this. I would close my eyes and imagine hearing the piano keys being played. I could feel the music I was creating, and I so loved the sounds in my head. I felt a great appreciation for this beauty of my imaginal sound. I could feel the keys under my agile fingers. I wasn't trying to manifest a piano. I was just enjoying the idea of playing one. The experience taught me a lot about manifestation because I was gifted with two pianos, unintentionally.

The combination of feeling and imagery worked the energy into a manifestation. You've probably heard of vision boards to make your dreams come true. Make sure you feel the reality of your vision too. I am also referring to healing energy work. When healing, you do the same thing. See the healing done. Feel it done. Feel healthy and full of vitality. See yourself as young and active. Feel what it's like to run through the forest! Whatever your favorite thing is, whatever brings you joy, feel and envision it. That is healing. Sometimes you have to take a sideways approach to illness. Bring in the joy, and illness cannot thrive. Rather than work at making the illness go away, which keeps your awareness on the illness, focus on what brings joy.

Receiving energy

People are sending and receiving energy all the time. Being aware of it is the tricky part. I have experienced others sending me some negative energy at times and have had different reactions to it. One story is someone that I set off a lot heard that I had written a book. This was a long time ago now, but at the time, I could hear her ranting through the planes for three days. I heard her statements such as: "That punk thinks she knows enough to write a book! She gets a Bachelor's degree and thinks she knows everything!" and on it went, for three days. At the time, I was pretty arrogant, being an Earth type, and I provoked her issues with her father and ex-husband, neither of whom would allow her to know more than them (also Earth types). So she ranted. I responded by remaining neutral within myself, allowing her the time to work it out. Had I engaged, even on the planes, it would have gone on longer. When she was done I sent her love energy to help soothe the activation.

I have a few stories like that, but I think you get the idea. Even if you think you are secretly being jealous, or petty, or whatever it is, it isn't likely a secret. People can feel you, and hear you on the planes. More and more are developing their intuitive skills. They know what you're doing.

Agreement, Shields, and Grounding

Sometimes people send you energy without your agreement. That's just human, much like the person I referred to in the previous story. If you are not aware of it, you might feel cranky, or anxious, or whatever and wonder why you feel that way. In the previous story I mentioned that I remained neutral so not to engage their energy in a negative way. I also did something else.

I used an energy shield to filter out her rants. A shield is the single most useful energy tool you can possibly learn, in my opinion. If you are feeling cranky, or anxious and you don't know why, put up a shield and see if it stops. If it does, the energy isn't yours. If it continues, it probably is yours and having a shield allows you to protect others from yourself.

Like all energy work, shields are a creative process. You can make a shield in any way that fits the situation. You begin by grounding yourself. Make sure that your root chakra cord is firmly attached to the earth. Imagine your feet ankle-deep in something that feels grounding. It could be red dirt, ocean water, rock, mud, or whatever works for you. Try different things to see what works. The same thing may not work for all situations. You can also ask Higher Self to show you what you need. I find that always works best. They know more than you.

Then you can begin to feel what the shield will do for you. What is needed here? I'll offer another story as an example. I was at a metaphysical fair, and a woman I know said to me that her business suffered because her energy seems off-putting to people, even though all she wants to do is help them. I knew what she meant because I had felt it from her too. She has a soft and loving interior, but an outer bubble of pure mental energy. To a bunch of intuitives who all feel energy, none often appreciate a pure mental state like hers. People who rely on feeling as their language don't appreciate not being able to feel others' emotions. I explained that to her, and she understood immediately and asked me what to do. I tried a couple of things that didn't feel right and then settled on a different approach. I tried a toric (donut-shaped) energy shield so that her inside softness could be projected outside of the mental layers that people were seeing. This meant that she could now be seen as a softer, more emotional person. I explained what I was doing so she could do it for herself, and it felt to me like a good solution. She took it around the event for a test drive and returned an hour later saying that it works and she just acquired two new clients.

Instructing your body

You have more control over your biology than you might realize. Biofeedback has shown that people can lower their heart rate, reduce pain, and more. How about sending love to your body? Messages of love can go a long way to healthy living. Tell your body to reproduce cells from when you were age 12 or 25, or whenever you felt the best.[19] Maybe tell your body what time of day to eliminate waste, or perhaps that it should accept what you are putting into it. Try different things that you can think of. The trick to them is to know with certainty that you are in charge. Use your power with intention and authority. Doubt is instinct taking control.

Please notice that I call this section instructing your body. You are the master. Your cells are waiting for you to give them directives. Respectfully and with gratitude for how it serves you, provide it with instructions. It is here to serve you. You are not your body. It is your vehicle for gaining experience of consciousness separation.

Your body always seeks balance. Your job is to provide it with the proper nutrients, exercise, and energy that it needs to thrive, and it will serve you a very long time, provided that you don't have a karmic issue to work out that involves something physical. Emotional energy can get stuck in your body, as I've pointed out previously. When I was working as a medical intuitive, I saw that people who run or do cardio-

---

[19] A Kryon idea.

type exercise on a regular basis had the least amount of stuck energy. It is possible to move emotional energy through physical movement. This does not mean that intense physical exercise will prevent you from developing disease because there are other reasons for disease besides emotional blockages. But physical exercise is a good thing. You were built for it.

Part 5: Summary of Mastery

Kryon has provided some attributes of mastery that I offer you here.
1. The ability to hold oneself at peace in the midst of turmoil. (I discussed this as placing your awareness in your heart center.) Yeshua and Buddha both spoke about fear.
2. The ability to observe without reacting to any given situation. What once provoked your instinctive reactivity will no longer do so.
3. You are able to hold so much light through peace and love that the darkness of dysfunction can no longer touch you. Other people can be how they want. It won't matter to you.
4. Mastery never diminishes another person through gossip, judgment, or disrespectful words.

I would add that masters know:
- How to partner with Gaia.
- How to work energy.
- That intuitive information is valid.
- How to sort their own instinctive perceptions from truthful intuitive information.
- How to interact with their body.
- How to hold their Gift of Grace.

Please keep in mind that mastery has to be chosen moment by moment because instinct is the default perception. The more practice you have, the easier it is to stay in wholeness because you will develop new neural pathways to accommodate your new perceptions.

Some symptoms of mastery:
- A desire to spend time outside with nature.
- A desire to spend time in meditation and intuitive

conditions.
- A desire to not watch TV or the news.
- A desire to eat fresh, whole food that is organic and free of nutrient-destroying chemicals.
- A desire to treat yourself and your body well, recognizing the value of balance in rest, inner processes, and outer activities.
- A stronger longing to spend time at home. Home means spirit. In this way, your home is always with you. It is comforting, soothing, and never far away.

Activity Suggestions

A few questions you could ask yourself to help you get going on mastery are:
1. What are your values? What matters most to you? You can use a mind map to help you prioritize these if that feels right for you.
2. In what ways do you sabotage your values?
3. In what ways do you live up to your values?
4. Define your ideal self.
5. Define your real self.
6. Where are these two selves in conflict? What areas can be changed? What areas must be accepted? If you can't change it, it must be accepted. If you can't accept it, it must be changed.
7. Where might you be denying responsibility for your life and what happens within it?
8. In what ways do you invite heaven into your psyche?
9. Does what you're doing serve higher self/God?

Thank you for working toward wholeness.
Please visit HumanADifferentWay.com

Appendix A: Thinking Words

Adapt	Convince	Identify	Predict
Analyze	Create	Illustrate	Prepare
Anticipate	Criticize	Indicate	Qualify
Apply	Decide	Infer	Quantify
Appraise	Defend	Integrate	Rank
Arrange	Define	Interpret	Rearrange
Assemble	Demonstrate	Invent	Recall
Assess	Describe	Judge	Recognize
Aware	Design	Label	Recommend
Calculate	Differentiate	List	Reframe
Change	Discern	Measure	Score
Choose	Discover	Memorize	Show
Classify	Discriminate	Modify	Solve
Collaborate	Discuss	Name	Structure
Compare	Estimate	Order	Summarize
Conclude	Evaluate	Organize	Summarize
Consider	Examine	Paraphrase	Support
Construct	Explain	Plan	Translate

Appendix B: Feeling Words

Accepting	Concerned	Doubt	Humiliated
Admiring	Confident	Dread	Hurt
Adorning	Conflicted	Eager	Impatient
Agitated	Confused	Elated	Inadequate
Alone	Connected	Embarrassed	Indifferent
Alone	Considerate	Empathy	Insecure
Amazed	Contempt	Empowered	Inspired
Ambitious	Content	Empty	Interested
Amused	Courageous	Encouraged	Intimidated
Angry	Creative	Energetic	Irritated
Anguished	Curious	Enthused	Jealous
Annoyed	Defeated	Envy	Kind
Anxiety	Defensive	Euphoria	Lonely
Appalled	Defensive	Excited	Longing
Apprehensive	Defiant	Fear	Loving
Awe	Denial	Fearless	Lucky
Bereaved	Depressed	Flustered	Moody
Betrayed	Despair	Focused	Motivated
Bitter	Desperate	Friendly	Moved
Bold	Determined	Gratitude	Neglected
Brave	Devastated	Grief	Nostalgic
Calm	Disgusted	Guilt	Numinous
Capable	Disappointed	Hatred	Obsessed
Certainty	Disbelief	Homesick	Optimistic
Chaotic	Discouraged	Hopeful	Overwhelmed
Comfortable	Disillusioned	Horified	Panic
Compassionate	Dissatisfied	Humbled	Peaceful

Pity	Resigned	Suspicious	Uneasy
Pleased	Ruined	Sympathetic	Unsafe
Powerless	Sad	Terrified	Unworthy
Prepared	Satisfied	Thankful	Validated
Prideful	Shame	Thoughtful	Valued
Rage	Shock	Tormented	Vengeful
Regretful	Shy	Trapped	Vindicated
Rejected	Skeptical	Trusting	Vulnerable
Relief	Smiley	Unappreciated	Wary
Remorseful	Smug	Uncertain	Worried
Resentful	Surprised	Understood	Worthless

Appendix C: The Enneagrid (not Enneagram)

The system of opposites in which your instinct perceptions reside may be related to numbers and nature. More research on this will be needed, but for now, I'd like to show you something about numbers that relates to the complexity of instinct templates.

There is large agreement that math is the language of the universe. Math can also be sound, as in music theory and frequency, but I am talking about actual multiplication, addition, subtraction, and the archetypal significance of numbers. Some would say that the idea I present here is meaningless because humans invented the numbers and counting systems. I say, humans are God and discover things more than they invent them as awareness taps into the unconscious where creation lives. Your belief system will determine the truth of it for you. However, regardless of what number or counting system has been created, the relationship of numbers to nature is proven through music, frequency, physics, fractals, and their archetypal condition.

The numbers 1-9 have some interesting characteristics that relate to the instinct patterns of perception and the alchemical concept of unity separating into the four classical elements. The number 9 stands out as unique among the digits. It stands complete unto itself, unaffected by the others. No matter what number is added to 9, that number remains intact. For example, $9 + 7$ is 16. $1 + 6 = 7$. 9 has no influence as though it is invisible or multi-dimensional. Nine acts like a mysterious stranger that you can see, but can't quite get to know. All multiples of 9 root to nine. For example, $9 \times 2 = 18$. $1 + 8 = 9$.

The digits 1-8 pair up to make 9. 1 and 8, 2 and 7, 3 and 6, and 4 and 5. Nine stands alone. It can be added to 0, but 0 accounts for the null, the nothingness, emptiness, while 9 stands for completion, totality, and cannot be affected by the other numbers. It is as if nine and zero act as the extreme ends of a linear spectrum of opposites.

I stated that the number system has an interesting characteristic that reflects the instinct template.

The standard multiplication table consists of digits set into a grid. Where the two numbers meet represents their product, or what they total when multiplied.

1	2	3	4	5	6	7	8	9	10	11	12	13	14	15
2	4	6	8	10	12	14	16	18	20	22	24	26	28	30
3	6	9	12	15	18	21	24	27	30	33	36	39	42	45
4	8	12	16	20	24	28	32	36	40	44	48	52	56	60
5	10	15	20	25	30	35	40	45	50	55	60	65	70	75
6	12	18	24	30	36	42	48	54	60	66	72	78	84	90
7	14	21	28	35	42	49	56	63	70	77	84	91	98	105
8	16	24	32	40	48	56	64	72	80	88	96	104	118	126
9	18	27	36	45	54	63	72	81	90	99	108	117	126	135
10	20	30	40	50	60	70	80	90	100	110	120	130	140	150
11	22	33	44	55	66	77	88	99	110	121	132	143	154	165
12	24	36	48	60	72	84	96	108	120	132	144	156	168	180
13	26	39	52	65	78	91	104	117	130	143	156	169	182	195
14	28	42	56	70	84	98	118	126	140	154	168	182	196	210
15	30	45	60	75	90	105	126	135	150	165	180	195	210	225

Numerologists, those who study the archetypal meaning of numbers, do something called rooting down a number. Rooting takes a multi-digit number and adds all digits together until a single digit is reached. For example, 12 is rooted as $1 + 2 = 3$. The rooted digit of 12 is 3.

I had recently learned about rooting when I found myself staring at a multiplication table in the back of a composition notebook in circa 2000. Out of curiosity, I began rooting in my head, and I thought something was

1	2	3	4	5	6	7	8	9	1	2	3	4	5	6
2	4	6	8	1	3	5	7	9	2	4	6	8	1	3
3	6	9	3	6	9	3	6	9	3	6	9	3	6	9
4	8	3	7	2	6	1	5	9	4	8	3	8	2	6
5	1	6	2	7	3	8	4	9	5	1	6	2	7	3
6	3	9	6	3	9	6	3	9	6	3	9	6	3	9
7	5	3	1	8	6	4	2	9	7	5	3	1	8	6
8	7	6	5	4	3	2	1	9	8	7	6	5	4	3
9	9	9	9	9	9	9	9	9	9	9	9	9	9	9
1	2	3	4	5	6	7	8	9	1	2	3	4	5	6
2	4	6	8	1	3	5	7	9	2	4	6	8	1	3
3	6	9	3	6	9	3	6	9	3	6	9	3	6	9
4	8	3	8	2	6	1	5	9	4	8	3	8	2	6
5	1	6	2	7	3	8	4	9	5	1	6	2	7	3
6	3	9	6	3	9	6	3	9	6	3	9	6	3	9

happening, but I couldn't tell what because I couldn't keep track of it all in my head. I got out some paper and made a grid of rooted-down digits. Something interesting was definitely happening.

The first thing I noticed was the number 9. It created a line around the numbers 1-8, much like a membrane around a cell. That nine-line, running in both directions, separated out the 1-8 numbers into a grid that repeated itself over and over. No matter how far out the numbers are multiplied, the same pattern repeats (like fractals). Nine remains within itself complete at all times, while at the same time, contains all the other digits within it through their pairings.

1	2	3	4	5	6	7	8	9	1	2	3	4	5	6
2	4	6	8	1	3	5	7	9	2	4	6	8	1	3
3	6	9	3	6	9	3	6	9	3	6	9	3	6	9
4	8	3	7	2	6	1	5	9	4	8	3	8	2	6
5	1	6	2	7	3	8	4	9	5	1	6	2	7	3
6	3	9	6	3	9	6	3	9	6	3	9	6	3	9
7	5	3	1	8	6	4	2	9	7	5	3	1	8	6
8	7	6	5	4	3	2	1	9	8	7	6	5	4	3
9	9	9	9	9	9	9	9	9	9	9	9	9	9	9
1	2	3	4	5	6	7	8	9	1	2	3	4	5	6
2	4	6	8	1	3	5	7	9	2	4	6	8	1	3
3	6	9	3	6	9	3	6	9	3	6	9	3	6	9
4	8	3	8	2	6	1	5	9	4	8	3	8	2	6
5	1	6	2	7	3	8	4	9	5	1	6	2	7	3
6	3	9	6	3	9	6	3	9	6	3	9	6	3	9

This led me to notice that the numbers do in fact pair up together: 1 and 8, 2 and 7, 3 and 6, and 4 and 5. I drew a heavy line between the 4 and 5 in both directions to sort out this paired perspective (Quadrants). Looking more deeply, I realized that the upper left quadrant exactly mirrors the lower right quadrant. The upper right exactly mirrors the lower left. The numbers remain paired in opposing columns and rows throughout the grid.

1	2	3	4	5	6	7	8
2	4	6	8	1	3	5	7
3	6	9	3	6	9	3	6
4	8	3	7	2	6	1	5
5	1	6	2	7	3	8	4
6	3	9	6	3	9	6	3
7	5	3	1	8	6	4	2
8	7	6	5	4	3	2	1

The unity of nine has separated into four opposites, or what alchemists call the four elements of fire, earth, air, and water. Also, the wholeness of 9 is reflected in each "cell" or quarter, like a nucleus. If you've read the section of this book on the instinct patterns, you would see the mirroring principle of opposites that are the two axes of water – fire, and earth – air. They too mirror each other, very much like our number system.

What is also known is that energy is frequency and frequency is geometric shape. When the number pairs are placed into a three-dimensional cube, with all six sides containing the grid, it becomes possible to connect all the number pairs together with lines. All the ones and all the eights work together to create a shape. So do the twos and sevens, and so on.

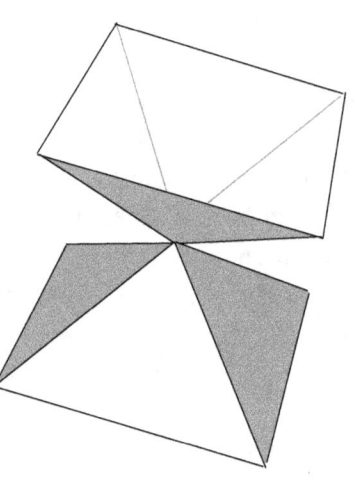

The 3 and 6 pair of numbers appears within the Enneagrid (as I call it) twice as often as the other numbers. Their geometric shape creates what is called Metatron's Cube.
There are other ways that these number shapes could be drawn. These are what

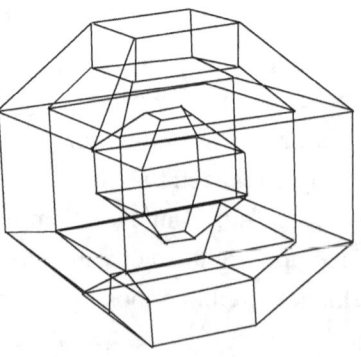

came out of me when I did it. Science knows that nature uses fractals to create matter in its rough irregular shapes such as rocks, trees, shorelines, mountains, the human nervous system, the human circulatory system, lungs, etc. The very egg that creates a human being begins as a single cell that when joined by an opposite force of sperm, begins to divide and multiply into more cells in a 2^x fashion. That is a fractal type of action.

The human psyche is not man-made. It is a product of nature and as such seems to be subject to how nature manifests matter. It stands to reason then that the instinct templates may be the energy of the material world of opposites. Through living a physical life, humans may be subject to physical conditions that include a perception of opposites.

Glossary

Archetype**: A structuring pattern within the collective unconscious that appears to us as an image of some kind. Images can be sounds, smells, visions, feelings, etc. Because they emerge from the collective unconscious, archetypes are common to all people regardless of race, religion or region. For example, all people understand a circle, square, father, mother, joker, magician, wise man, healer, counting, speaking, dreaming, etc.

Action Task: The action needed to begin overcoming instinct and work toward higher self integration.

Addictive Response: A behavioral compensation to the Core Perception.

Binary: Refers to the duality principle of energy dynamics, which comprise opposites, such as Masculine-feminine, up-down, hot-cold, in-out, back-forth, black-white, etc. The binary is the first division of energy (2^1) as it separates from wholeness, much like a human egg begins as a single cell and divides into two cells, then four, then eight and so on in a linear bifurcation that can be mathematically represented as 2^x.

Awareness Focus: For the cognitive portion of the Archedomi system, the Awareness Focus is the first action upon which you can actively place your efforts to begin moving your psyche into a multi-dimensional problem solving tool.

Boundaries: Boundaries occur both as inner experience and outer behavior.

<u>Inner experience</u>: Boundaries with yourself is an action of self-discipline. You stop yourself from eating too much, or over-staying your welcome, or _____.
<u>Outer behavior:</u> Boundaries used on the outside are those you set for others and how they interact with you. How much you will or won't tolerate of others behaviors.

Compensation: Like all products of nature, the psyche seeks balance. It does this through the binary system in which the ego/instinct exists. For example, if you have a need to think very highly of yourself, you might deny that others could possibly think ill of you. Denial compensates for the psyche's inability to accept its personality flaws.

Complex**: A complex is a feeling that creates an uncontrollable reaction to an activating stimulus. Jung saw the complex as a "splinter personality" as if another personality suddenly takes over and causes people to behave in ways they normally wouldn't. There are complexes that derive from environmental experiences, such as PTSD or childhood traumas, etc. (Also see Core Complex).

Complexity: Complexity occurs in two forms, as applied to Archedomi: linear and non-linear.
- The instinct patterns are <u>linear</u> and based on fractal formations that occur in a 2^x delineation much like cellular division of a human egg in that one (unity) divides into 2 (polarity), then four, eight, and so on.
- Higher self is <u>non-linear</u> and multidimensional. It has no linear pattern and therefore must be chosen in every moment. It is always available, but not always acquired.

Consciousness: Traditionally, this word is used to connote being aware of one's surroundings in the mundane world, aware of thoughts, feelings, and sensations. I understand that physicists are coming to believe that consciousness is the only thing that truly exists. It is the field of energy that is part of everything. Therefore I use the terms hidden (to denote the traditional idea of unconscious) and aware.

Core Complex: In the Archedomi model, the Core Complex is similar to Jung's definition of a complex, but it is imprinted at birth and acts as a driver for ego to function in survival mode. The Core Complex is not created through environmental experiences such as childhood traumas. That is more of a Jungian type of complex.

Core Perception: The feelings driven by the Core Complex of which you are aware. The Core Perception is your predominant experience and biggest fear that drives behavioral compensations. For example, If your Core Perception is rejection, you will compensate with behaviors of neediness and withdrawal, as well as striving to connect through emotional intensity.

Fractal: The resulting rough and irregular shape due to the reiteration of a simple quadratic equation. The shape retains its structure no matter how many reiterations are input once the shape is established.

Gift of Grace: A new inner state of being that arises from the inner action of the Awareness Focus and the outer behavior of the Positive Force.

Higher Self** : The part of you that sees multi-dimensionally and belongs to home (heaven), which is a state of being rather than a place.

Instinct/Ego/: The small self. It sees two-dimensionally meaning us-them, win-lose, compete-cooperate, etc.

Positive Force: A new outer behavior that arises as a result of taking inner action through the Awareness Focus.

Psyche: Psyche is from Greek and means soul. It is the animating invisible force that occupies a physical body. The body serves as a vehicle for psyche to exist.

Shadow**: A part of psyche that contains the unwanted parts of self and is part of the personal unconscious. If you deny some attribute of yourself that you don't like, it is hidden from your awareness in the shadow. Others may see your shadow side though.

Bibliography

Andrews, T. 2002. Animal Speak. Llewellyn Publications

Andrews, T. 2010. Animal Wise. DragonHawk

Anthony, C. K. 1988. A Guide to the I-Ching: 3rd Ed. Anthony Publishing Company. Stow: MA

Campbell, G. n.d. Empedocles. In Internet Encyclopedia of Philosophy. Retrieved from http://www.iep.utm.edu/empedocl/

Douglas-Klotz, N. 2022. Revelations of the Aramaic Jesus: The Hidden Teaching on Life and Death. Charlottsville, VA. Hampton Roads Publishing

Goulston, M. 2010. Psychology Today. Mirror Neuron Receptor Deficit: An Idea Whose Time Has Come. Retrieved from: https://www.psychologytoday.com/intl/blog/just-listen/201002/mirror-neuron-receptor-deficit-mnrd-idea-whose-time-has-come#:~:text=Mirror%20Neuron%20Receptor%20Deficit%2C%20Narcissism,t%20fly%20into%20a%20rage

Jung, C. G. 1935. Collected Works of C. G. Jung. Vol. 18. The Tavistock Lectures. Lecture III.

Jung, C. G. 1960. The collected works of C. G. Jung. Vol. 3. The Psychogenesis of Mental Disease: Recent Thoughts on Schizophrenia. Princeton, NJ: Princeton University Press. (Original work published 1956)

Jung, C. G. 1967. The collected works of C. G. Jung. Vol. 13. Alchemical studies. Princeton, NJ: Princeton University Press. (Original work published 1929)

Jung, C. G. 1981. The collected works of C. G. Jung. Vol. 8. Synchronicity: An acausal connecting principle. Princeton, NJ: Princeton University Press. (Original work published 1927)

Jung, C. G. 1990. The collected works of C. G. Jung. Vol. 9i. Archetypes of the collective unconscious. Princeton, NJ: Princeton University Press. (Original work published 1934)

Kalei'iliahi, Kahuna. 2016. Wisdom of the Ancestors: Messages from the Ancients. NP

King James Bible. 2021. Nashville, TN: Thomas Nelson. (Original work published 1769)

Nanamoli, B [Trans.]. Bodhi, B. [Ed.]. 2005. Majjhima Nikaya: The Middle Length Discourses of the Buddha. Somerville, MA: Wisdom Publications

Muranyi, M. 2013. The Gaia Effect: The Remarkable System of Collaboration Between Gaia and Humanity. Quebec, Canada: Ariane Publishing

Myss, C. 2013. Archetypes: Who Are You? Macon, GA. Hay House Publishing

Myss, C. 1996. Anatomy of the Spirit: The Seven Stages of Power and Healing. New York, NY: Harmony Books

Newhouse, E. 2012. Our Plastic Brain. https://www.psychologytoday.com/us/blog/invisible-wounds/201201/our-plastic-brain

Samuels, A., Shorter, B., & Plaut, F. 2003. A critical dictionary of Jungian analysis. New York, NY: Routledge

Tzu, L. 1919. Tao Te Ching (D. Goddard Trans.). Compromise Press

www.ingramcontent.com/pod-product-compliance
Lightning Source LLC
Chambersburg PA
CBHW052147070526
44585CB00017B/2007